For Engineers & Designers

BricsCAD Exercises

200 3D PRACTICE DRAWINGS

SACHIDANAND JHA

cadin360°
Learning Tutorials

Dear Reader,

Thank you for choosing **BricsCAD Exercises** book. This book is part of a family of premium-quality CADIN360 books, all of which are written by Outstanding author who combine practical experience with a gift for teaching.

CADIN360 was founded in 2016. More than 3 years later, we're still committed to producing consistently exceptional books. With each of our titles, we're working hard to set a new standard for the industry. From the paper we print on, to the authors we work with, our goal is to bring you the best books available.

I hope you see all that reflected in these pages. I'd be very interested to hear your comments and get your feedback on how we're doing. Feel free to let me know what you think about this or any other CADIN360 book by sending me an email at contactus@cadin360.com.

If you think you've found a technical error in this book, please visit
https://cadin360.com/contact-us/.
Customer feedback is critical to our efforts at CADIN360.

Best regards,

Sachidanand Jha
Founder & CEO, CADIN360

BricsCAD Exercises

Preface

BricsCAD Exercises

❖ This book contain 200 CAD practice exercises and drawings.

❖ This book does not provide step by step tutorial to design 3D models.

❖ S.I Unit is used.

❖ Predominantly used Third Angle Projection.

❖ This book is for **BricsCAD** and Other Feature-Based Modeling Software such as Inventor, SolidWorks, NX, Solid Edge, AutoCAD, PTC Creo etc.

❖ It is intended to provide Drafters, Designers and Engineers with enough 3D CAD exercises for practice on **BricsCAD**.

❖ It includes almost all types of exercises that are necessary to provide, clear, concise and systematic information required on industrial machine part drawings.

❖ Third Angle Projection is intentionally used to familiarize Drafters, Designers and Engineers in Third Angle Projection to meet the expectation of world wide Engineering drawing print.

❖ Clear and well drafted drawing help easy understanding of the design.

❖ This book is for Beginner, Intermediate and Advance CAD users.

❖ These exercises are from Basics to Advance level.

❖ Each exercises can be assigned and designed separately.

❖ No Exercise is a prerequisite for another. All dimensions are in mm.

❖ Note: Assume any missing dimensions.

EX-01

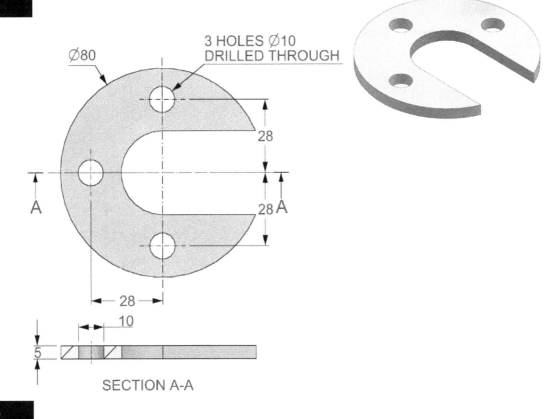

∅80

3 HOLES ∅10
DRILLED THROUGH

28

28 A

A

28

10

5

SECTION A-A

EX-02

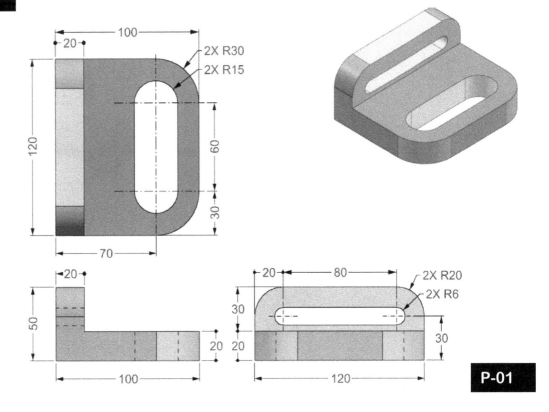

100

20

2X R30

2X R15

120

60

30

70

20

50

100

20

20 20

20

80

2X R20

2X R6

30

30

120

P-01

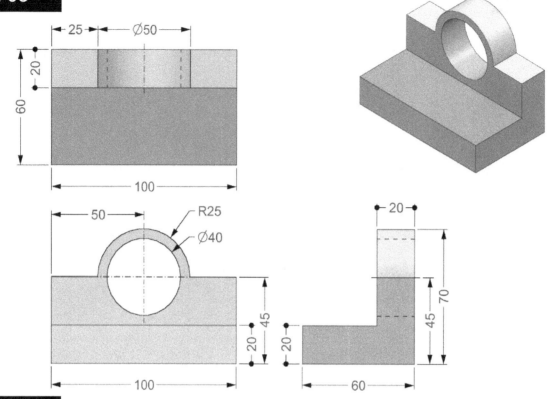

25 — Ø50
20
60
100

50 — R25
Ø40
45
20
100

20
70
45
20
60

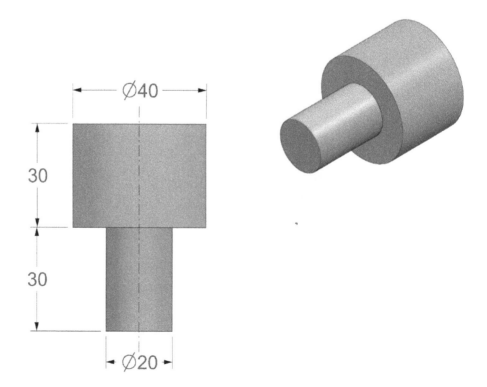

Ø40
30
30
Ø20

EX-05

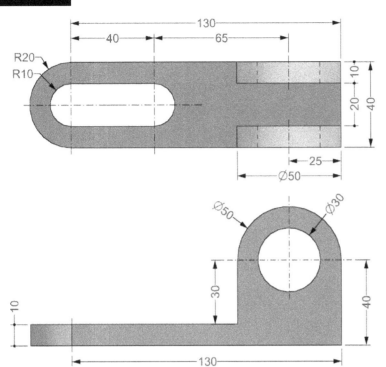

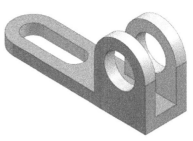

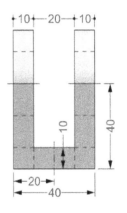

EX-06

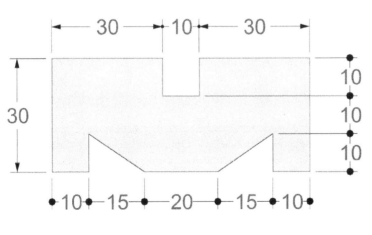

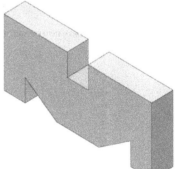

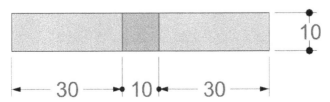

EX-07

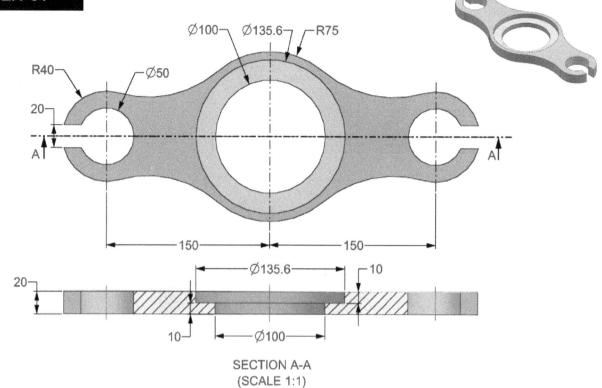

Ø100 Ø135.6 R75
R40 Ø50
20
A
A
150 150

Ø135.6 10
20
10 Ø100

SECTION A-A
(SCALE 1:1)

EX-08

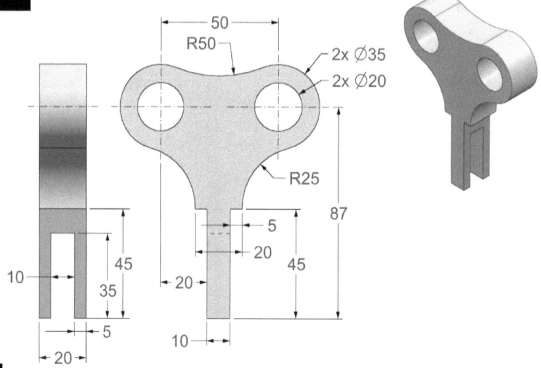

50
R50
2x Ø35
2x Ø20
R25
87
5
20
45
20
20
45
10
10
35
5
20

P-04

EX-09

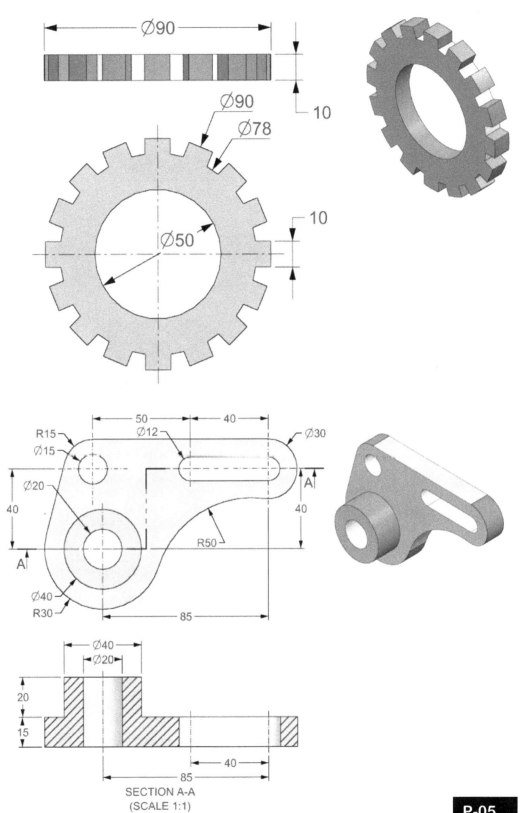

Ø90

10

Ø90
Ø78
10
Ø50

EX-10

50
40
R15
Ø12
Ø30
Ø15
Ø20
40
40
A
A
R50
R30
Ø40
85

Ø40
Ø20
20
15
40
85

SECTION A-A
(SCALE 1:1)

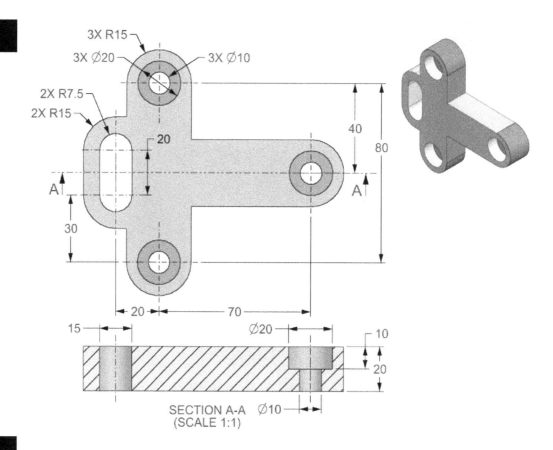

3X R15
3X Ø20
3X Ø10
2X R7.5
2X R15
20
40
80
A
30
20
70

15
Ø20
10
20

SECTION A-A
(SCALE 1:1)
Ø10

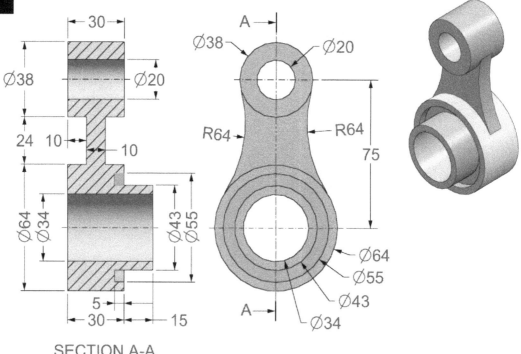

30
Ø38
Ø20
24 10
10
Ø64
Ø34
Ø43
Ø55
5
30
15

A
Ø38
Ø20
R64
R64
75
Ø64
Ø55
Ø43
Ø34
A

SECTION A-A
(SCALE 1:1)

EX-13

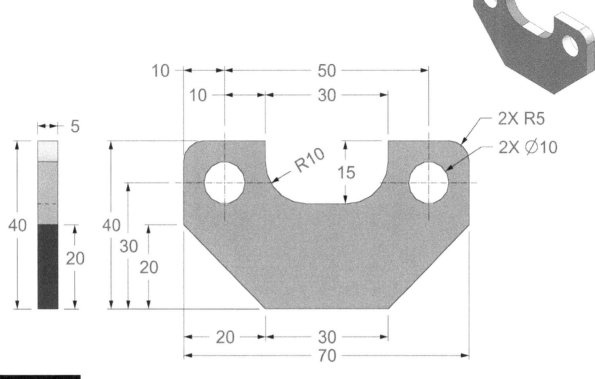

- 10
- 50
- 10
- 30
- 2X R5
- 2X Ø10
- R10
- 15
- 5
- 40
- 20
- 40
- 30
- 20
- 20
- 30
- 70

EX-14

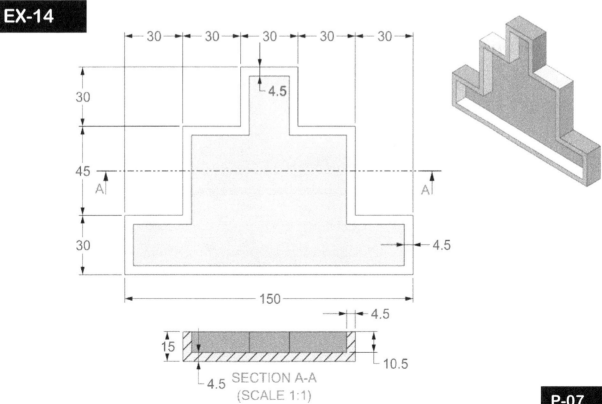

- 30
- 30
- 30
- 30
- 30
- 4.5
- 30
- 45
- A
- A
- 30
- 4.5
- 150
- 4.5
- 15
- 10.5
- 4.5

SECTION A-A
(SCALE 1:1)

P-07

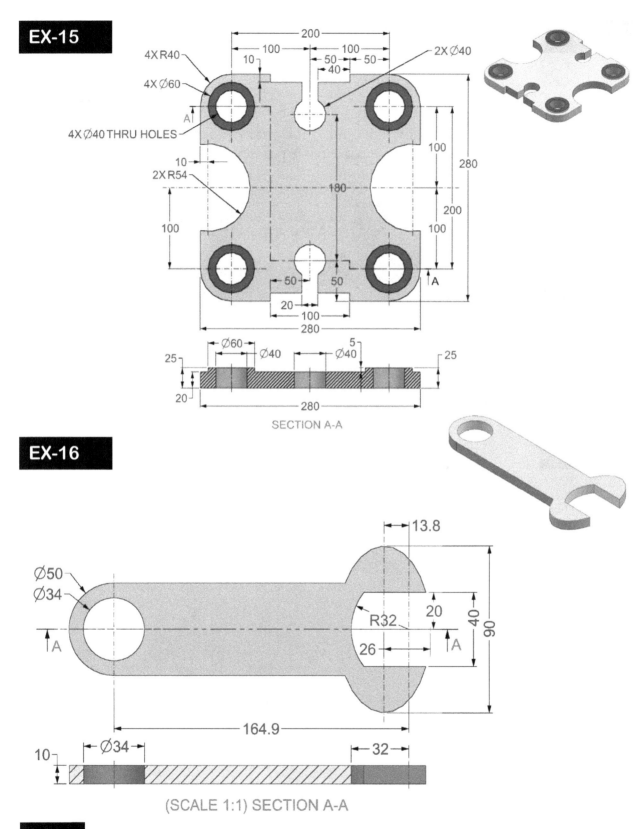

EX-15

4X R40
4X Ø60
4X Ø40 THRU HOLES
2X Ø40
2X R54

200
100
100
10
50
50
40
280
100
100
180
200
100
100
50
50
20
100
280

A

SECTION A-A

25
Ø60
Ø40
Ø40
5
25
20
280

EX-16

Ø50
Ø34
13.8
20
R32
40
90
26
A
A
164.9

10
Ø34
32

(SCALE 1:1) SECTION A-A

P-08

EX-17

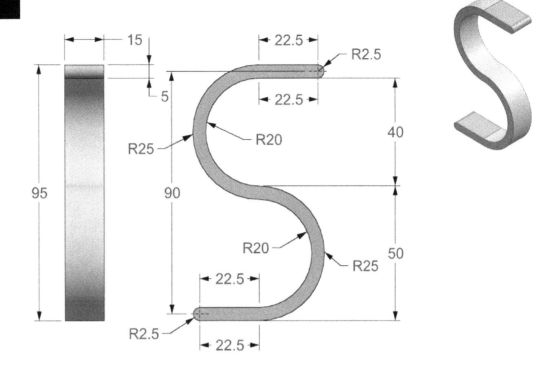

15
5
R2.5
22.5
22.5
R25
R20
95
40
90
R20
R25
50
22.5
R2.5
22.5

EX-18

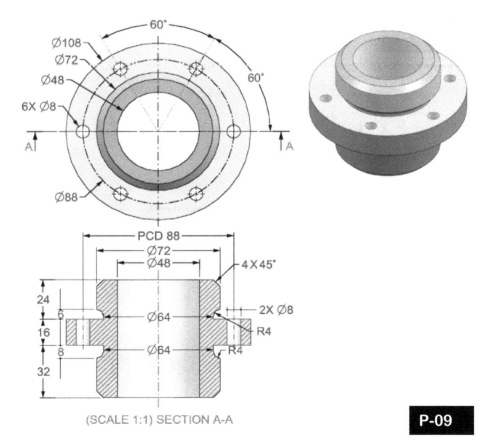

60°
Ø108
Ø72
Ø48
60°
6X Ø8
A
A
Ø88

PCD 88
Ø72
Ø48
4 X 45°
24
6
2X Ø8
Ø64
16
R4
8
Ø64
R4
32

(SCALE 1:1) SECTION A-A

P-09

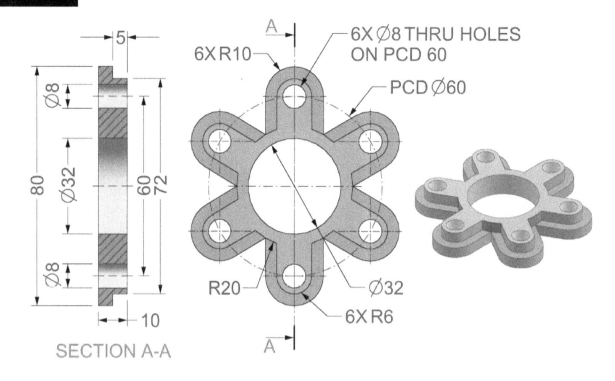

6X R10

6X Ø8 THRU HOLES ON PCD 60

PCD Ø60

Ø8
Ø32
Ø8
80
60
72
5
10

R20
Ø32
6X R6

SECTION A-A

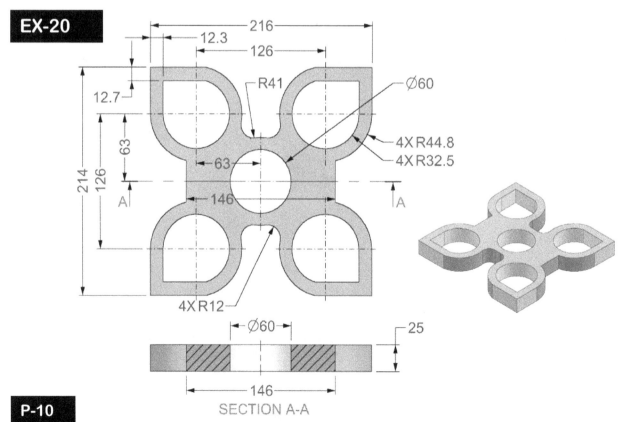

216
12.3
126
R41
Ø60
12.7
63
63
146
214
126
4X R44.8
4X R32.5
4X R12

Ø60
25
146

SECTION A-A

EX-21

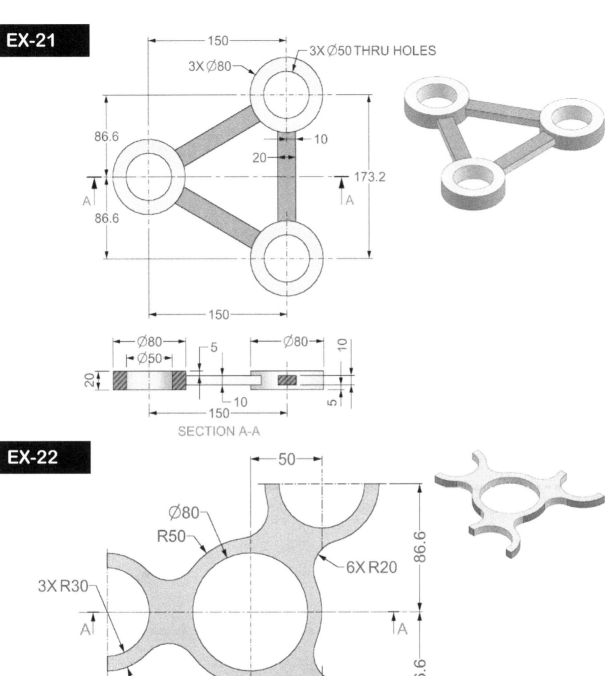

150
3X Ø50 THRU HOLES
3X Ø80
86.6
10
20
173.2
A
86.6
A
150

Ø80
Ø50
5
Ø80
10
20
10
150
5

SECTION A-A

EX-22

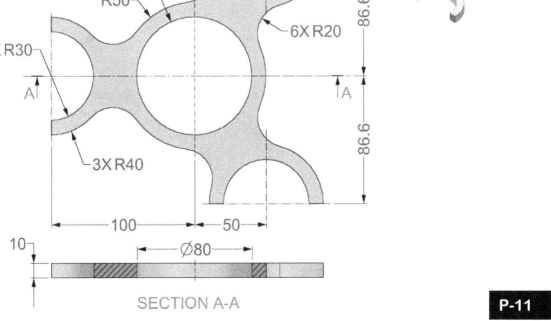

50
Ø80
R50
86.6
6X R20
3X R30
A
A
3X R40
86.6
100
50

10
Ø80

SECTION A-A

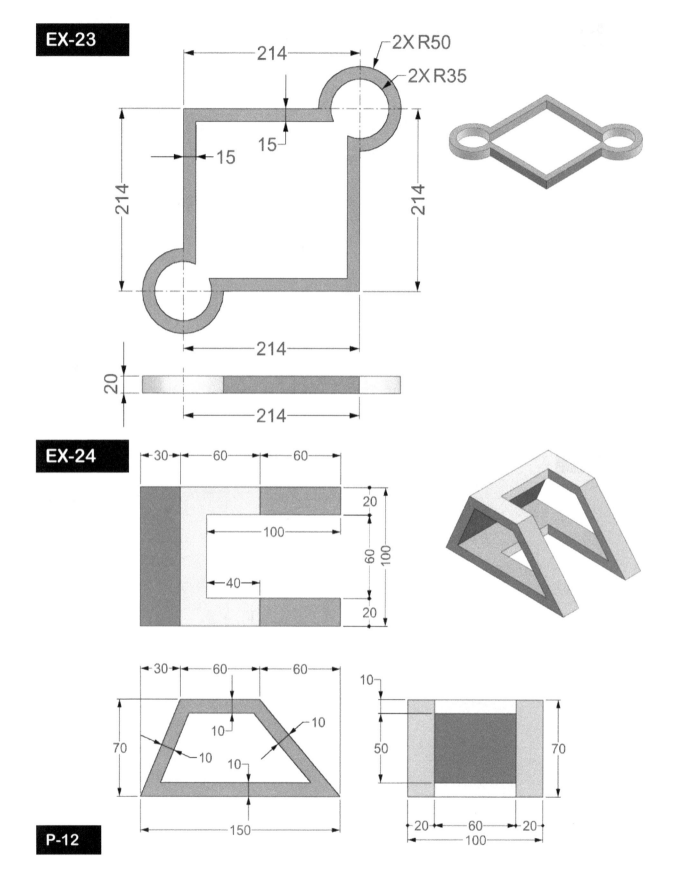

EX-23

214

2X R50

2X R35

15

15

214

214

214

20

214

EX-24

30

60

60

20

100

60

100

40

20

P-12

30

60

60

10

10

10

10

10

70

150

10

50

70

20

60

20

100

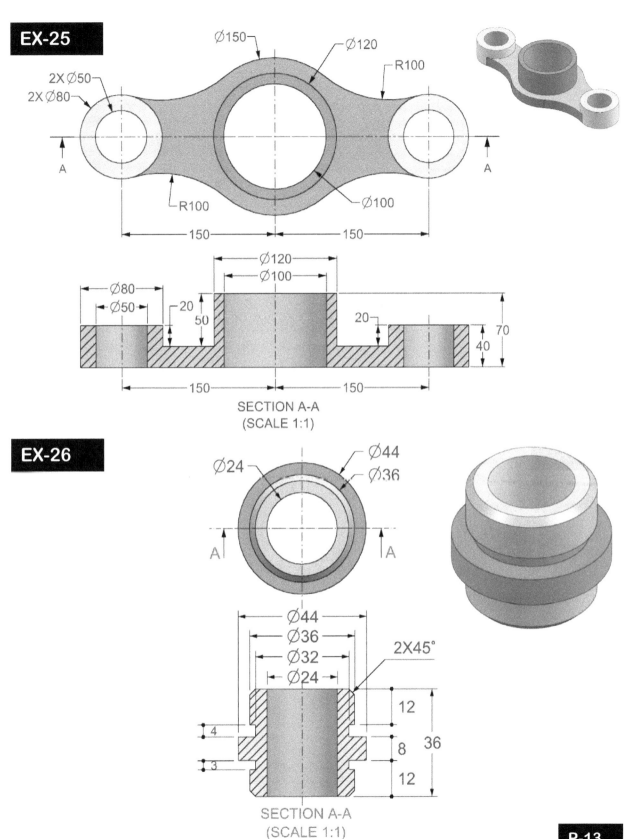

EX-25

Ø150
Ø120
R100
2X Ø50
2X Ø80
Ø100
R100
150
150

Ø120
Ø100
Ø80
Ø50
20
50
20
70
40
150
150

SECTION A-A
(SCALE 1:1)

EX-26

Ø24
Ø44
Ø36

A A

Ø44
Ø36
Ø32
Ø24
2X45°
12
4
8
36
3
12

SECTION A-A
(SCALE 1:1)

EX-27

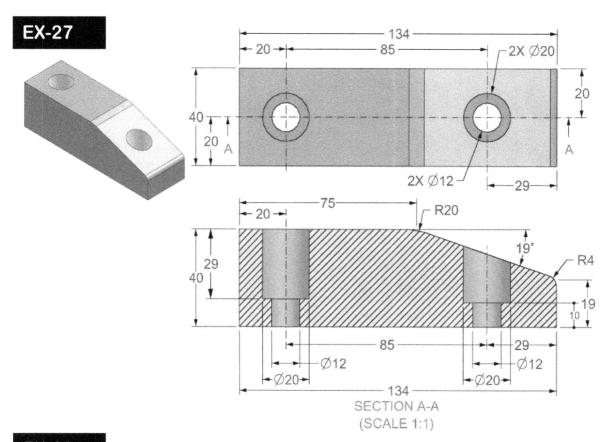

134
20
85
2X Ø20
20
40
20
A
A
2X Ø12
29

20
75
R20
19°
R4
29
40
19
10
85
29
Ø12
Ø12
Ø20
Ø20
134

SECTION A-A
(SCALE 1:1)

EX-28

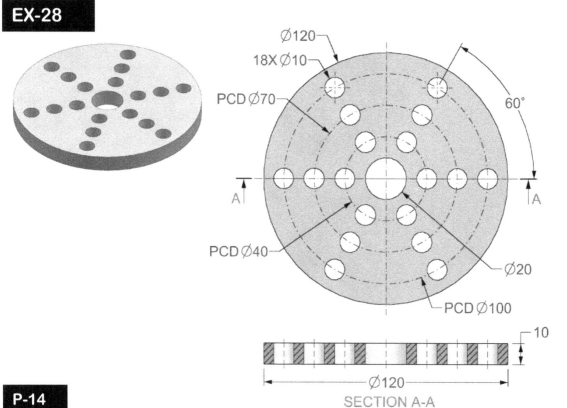

Ø120
18X Ø10
60°
PCD Ø70
A
A
PCD Ø40
Ø20
PCD Ø100

10
Ø120
SECTION A-A

P-14

EX-29

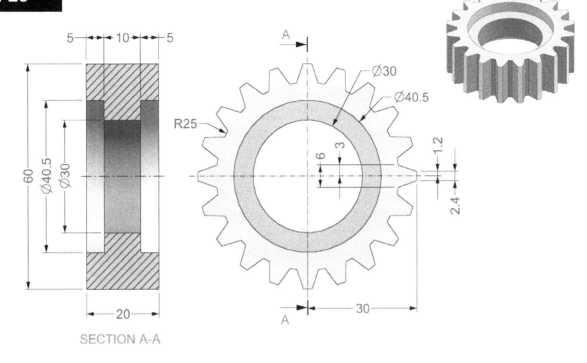

SECTION A-A

EX-30

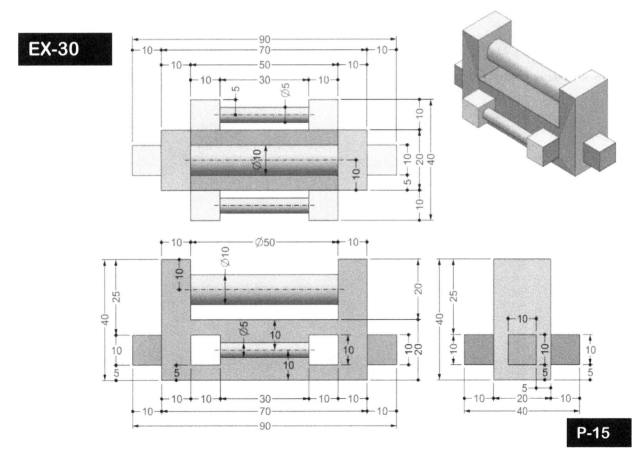

P-15

EX-31

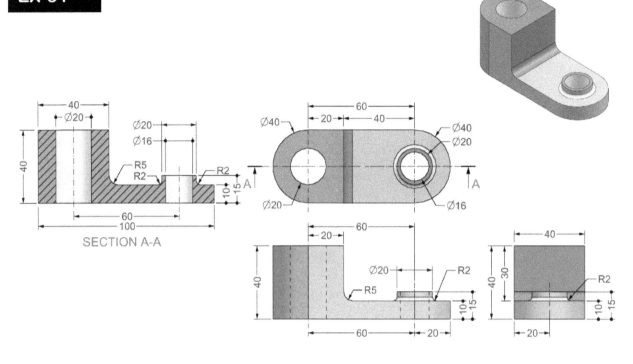

SECTION A-A

EX-32

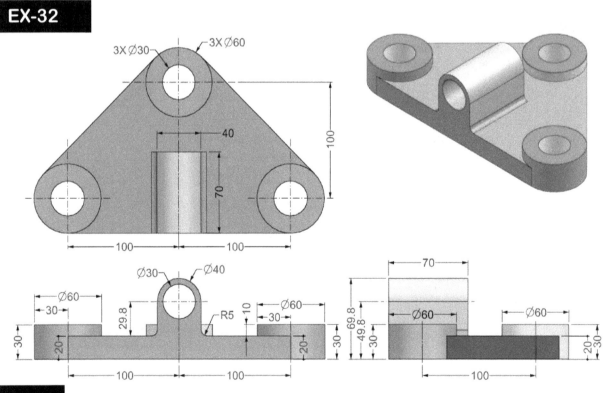

P-16

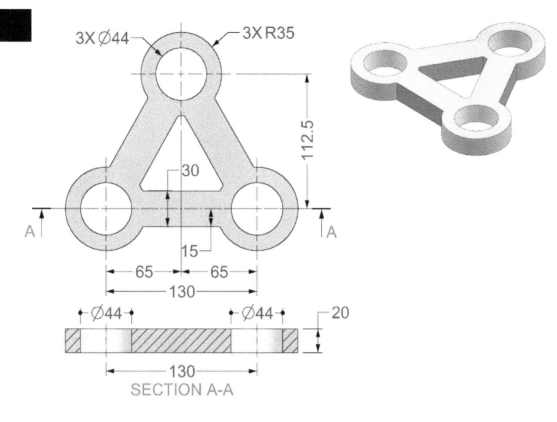

3X Ø44 — 3X R35

112.5

30

15

65 — 65

130

Ø44 — Ø44 — 20

130

SECTION A-A

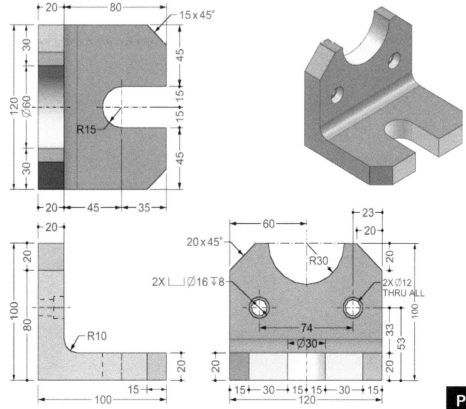

20 — 80 — 15 x 45°

30

45

120 Ø60

15

15

R15

30

45

20 — 45 — 35

20

20

100

80

R10

20

15

100

60 — 23

20 x 45° 20

R30

2X ⌴ Ø16 ⊤8

2X Ø12
THRU ALL

74

20

Ø30

33

53

20

15 — 30 — 15 — 15 — 30 — 15

120

100

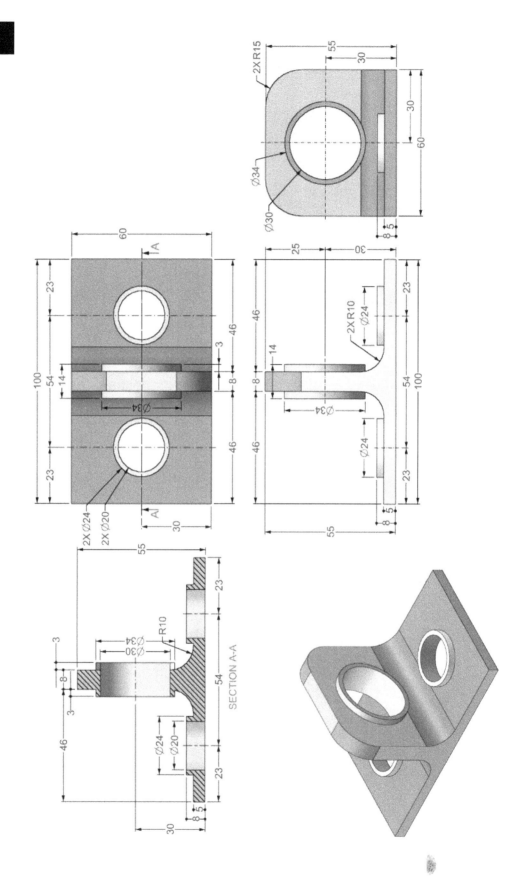

2X R15
55
30
30
60
Ø34
Ø30
8
5

60
A
23
46
3
100
54
14
8
Ø34
23
30
A
2X Ø24
2X Ø20

25
30
46
14
2X R10
Ø24
23
8
Ø34
54
100
Ø24
46
23
5
8
55

55
3
Ø34
R10
Ø30
8
23
54
3
46
Ø24
Ø20
23
5
8
30
SECTION A-A

EX-36

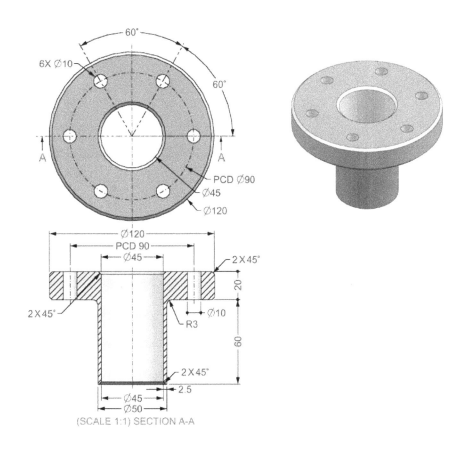

6X Ø10
60°
60°
PCD Ø90
Ø45
Ø120

A — A

Ø120
PCD 90
Ø45
2 X 45°
20
2 X 45°
Ø10
R3
60
2 X 45°
2.5
Ø45
Ø50

(SCALE 1:1) SECTION A-A

EX-37

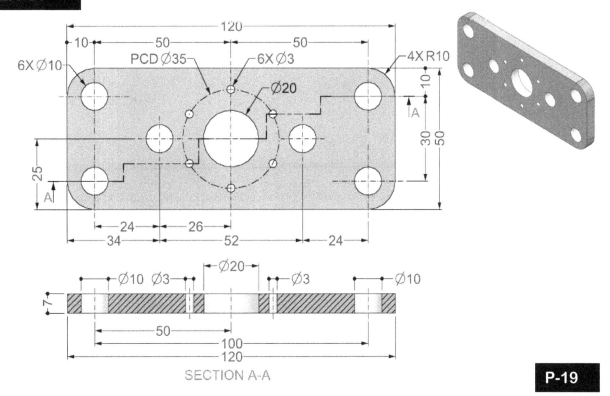

120
10
50
50
6X Ø10
PCD Ø35
6X Ø3
4X R10
Ø20
10
A
30
50
25
A
24
26
52
24
34

Ø10 Ø3
Ø20
Ø3
Ø10
7
50
100
120

SECTION A-A

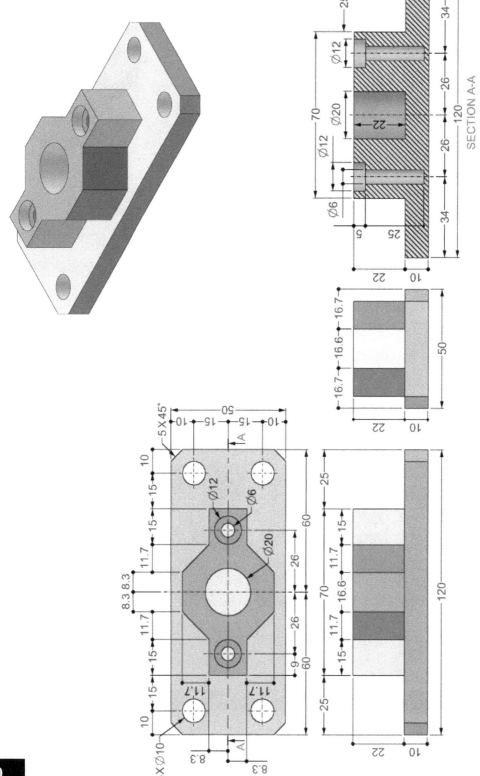

SECTION A-A

EX-39

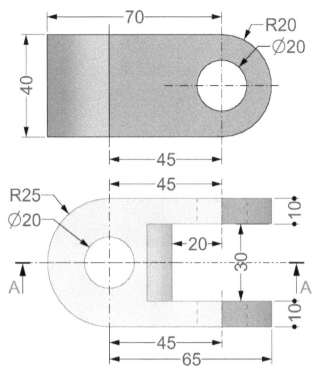

70

R20
Ø20

40

45

45

R25
Ø20

20

30

10

10

A

A

45

65

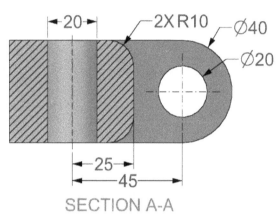

20

2X R10

Ø40

Ø20

25

45

SECTION A-A

EX-40

Ø60

20

10

5

Ø50

Ø60
Ø50

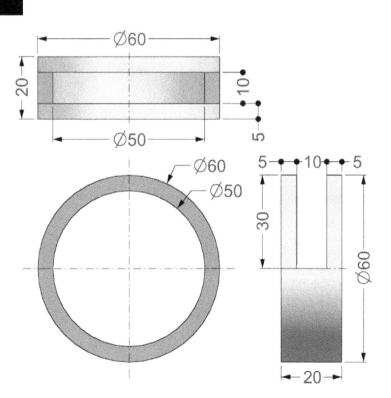

5 10 5

30

Ø60

20

P-21

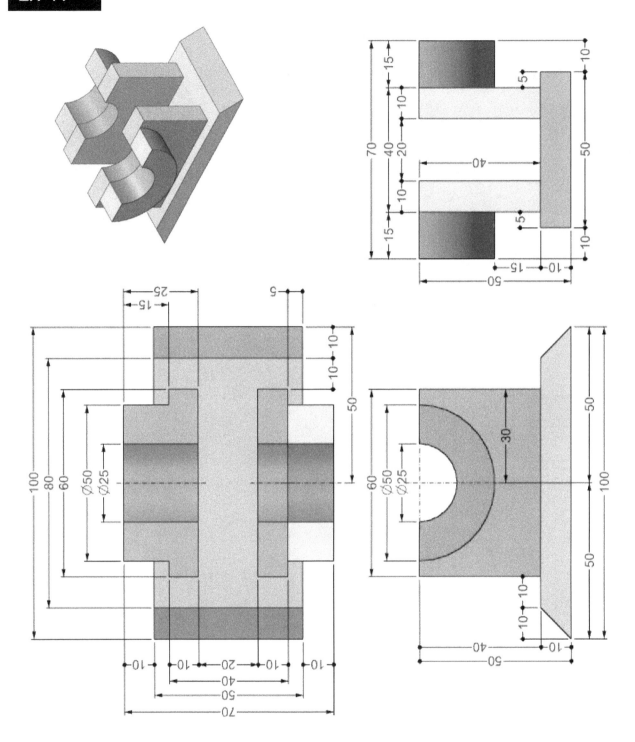

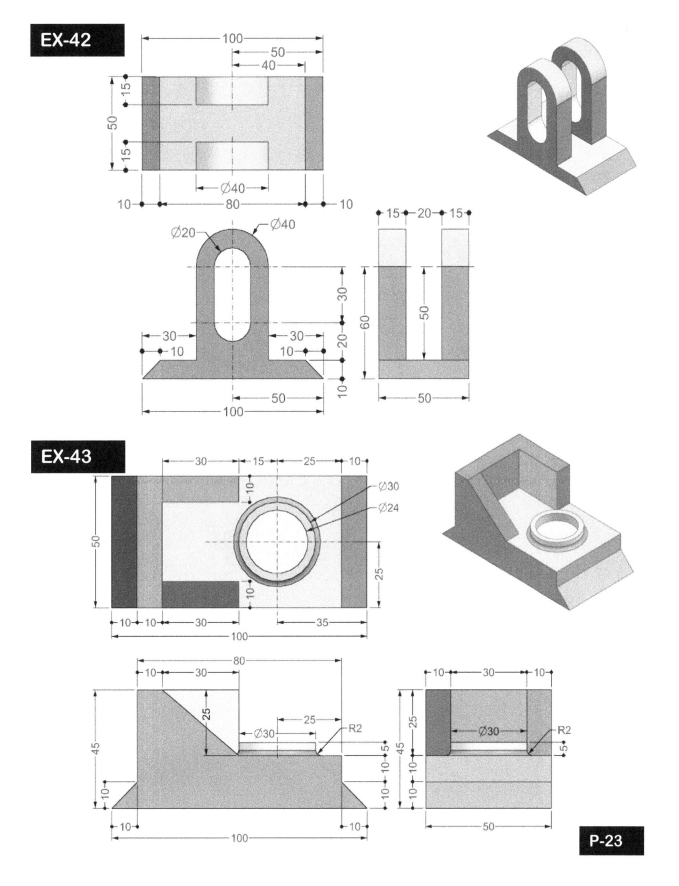

EX-42

EX-43

P-23

EX-44

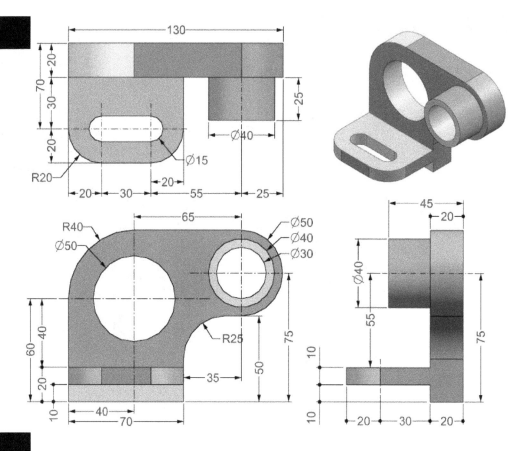

EX-45

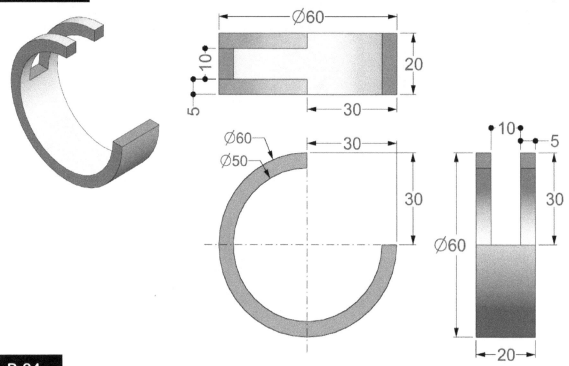

EX-46

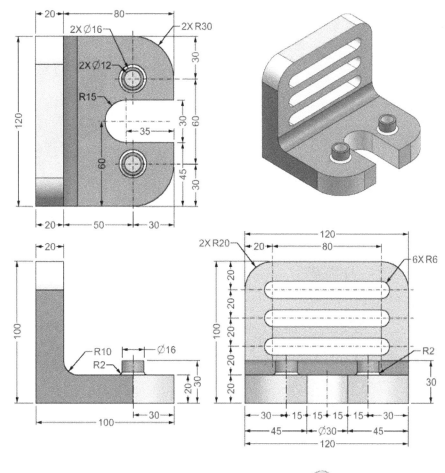

EX-47

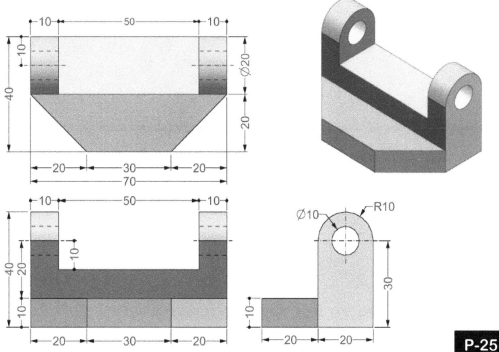

EX-48

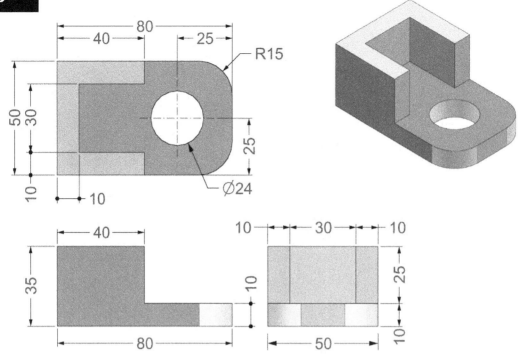

EX-49

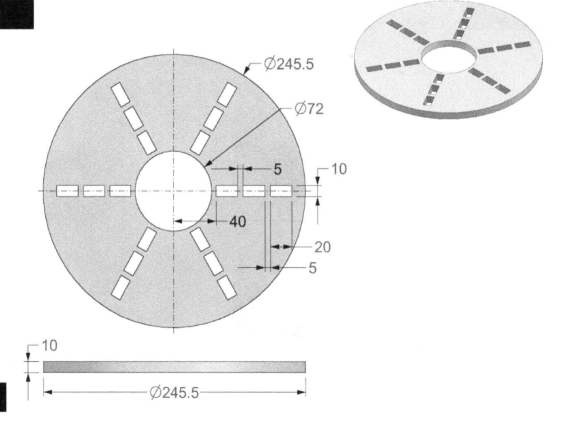

P-26

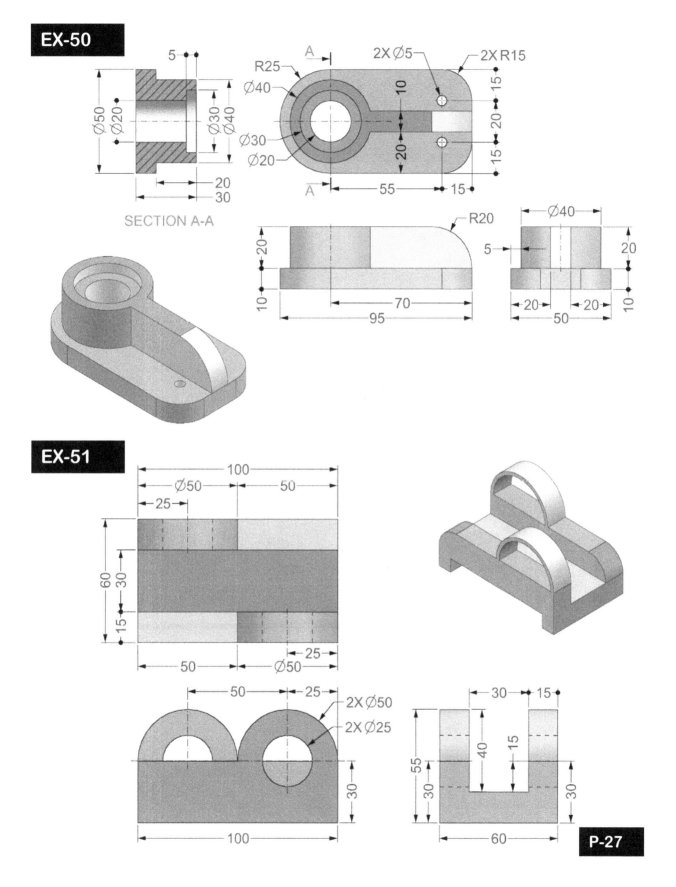

EX-50

R25
Ø40
Ø30
Ø20

5
Ø50
Ø20
Ø30
Ø40

20
30

SECTION A-A

A
2X Ø5
2X R15
10
15
20
15
20
55
15

R20
Ø40
5
20
20
10

20
10
70
95
50
20
20

EX-51

100
Ø50
50
25
60
30
15
50
Ø50
25

50
25
2X Ø50
2X Ø25
30
100

30
15
55
40
15
30
30
60

P-27

EX-52

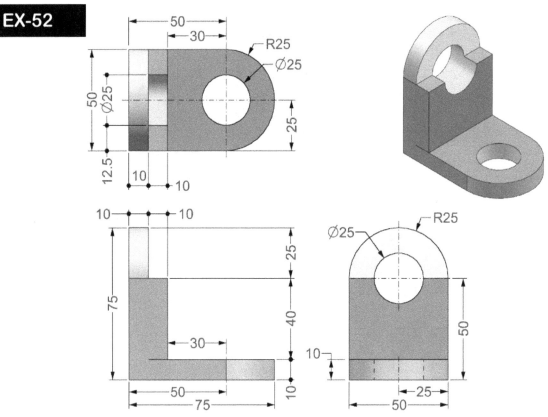

EX-53

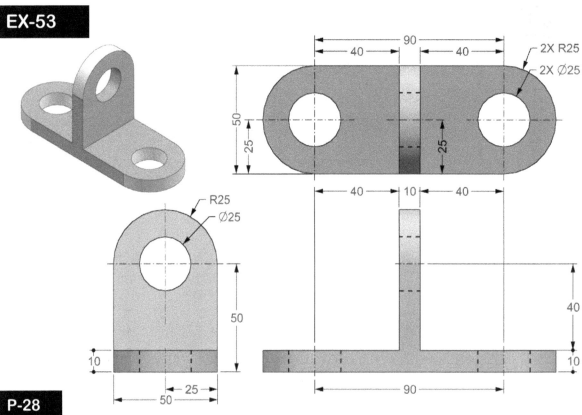

P-28

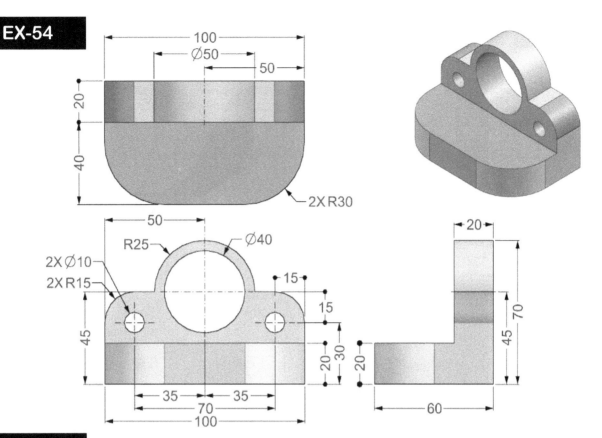

EX-54 drawing dimensions:
- 100
- Ø50
- 50
- 20
- 40
- 2X R30
- 50
- R25
- Ø40
- 2X Ø10
- 2X R15
- 15
- 15
- 45
- 30
- 20
- 20
- 35
- 35
- 70
- 100
- 20
- 70
- 45
- 60

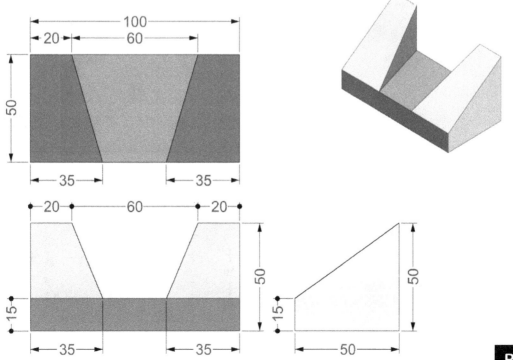

EX-55 drawing dimensions:
- 100
- 20
- 60
- 50
- 35
- 35
- 20
- 60
- 20
- 50
- 15
- 35
- 35
- 50
- 15
- 50

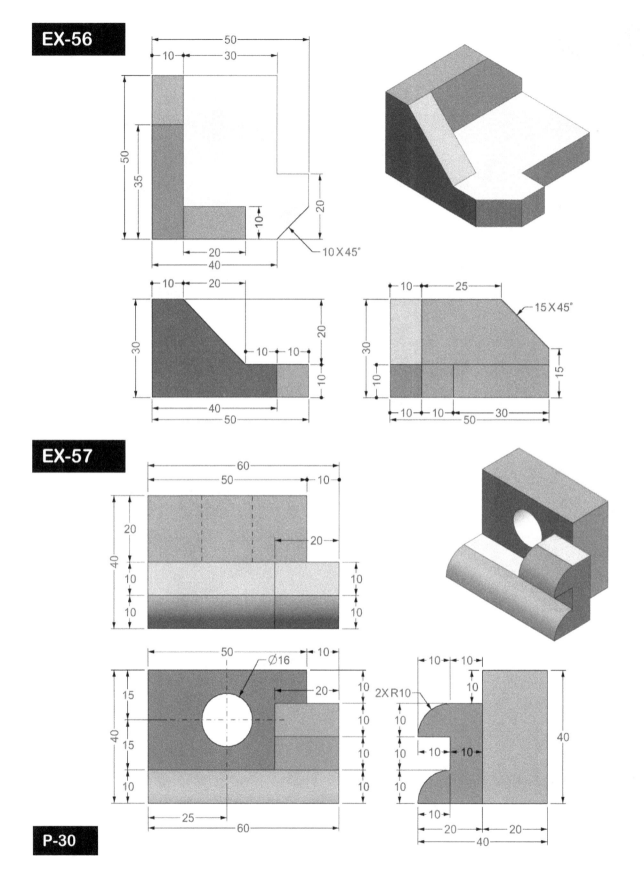

EX-56

50
10 30
50
35
20
10
10 X 45°
20
40

10 20
30
20
10 10
10
40
50

10 25
15 X 45°
30
10
15
10 10 30
50

EX-57

60
50 10
20
40
20
10 10
10 10

50 Ø16
10
15 20 10
40 10
15 10
10 10
25 10
60

10 10
10
2X R10
10
10 10
10
10
10 40
10
20 20
40

P-30

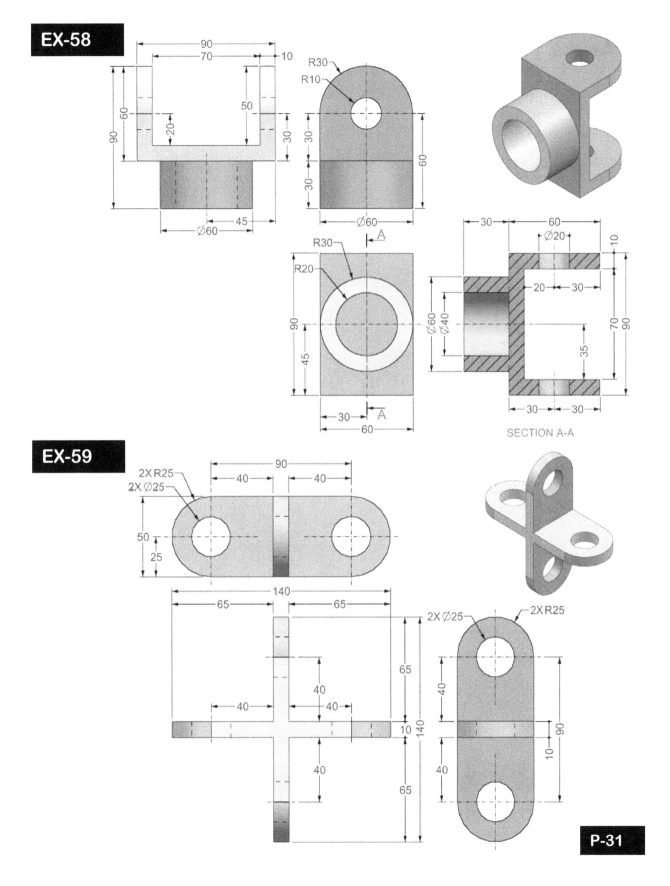

EX-58

R30
R10
90
70
10
60
50
20
30
90
30
45
Ø60

R30
Ø60
30
30
60

A

R30
R20
90
45
30
60
A

30
60
Ø20
20
30
10
Ø60
Ø40
70
90
35
30
30

SECTION A-A

EX-59

2X R25
2X Ø25
90
40
40
50
25

140
65
65
65
40
40
40
10
40
65

2X Ø25
2X R25
40
40
90
10

P-31

SECTION A-A

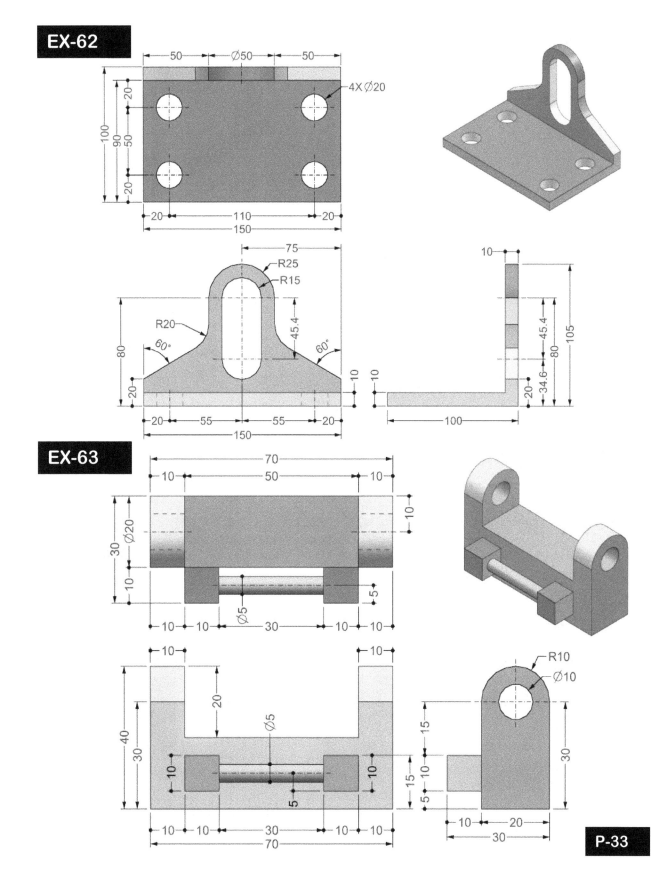

EX-62

EX-63

P-33

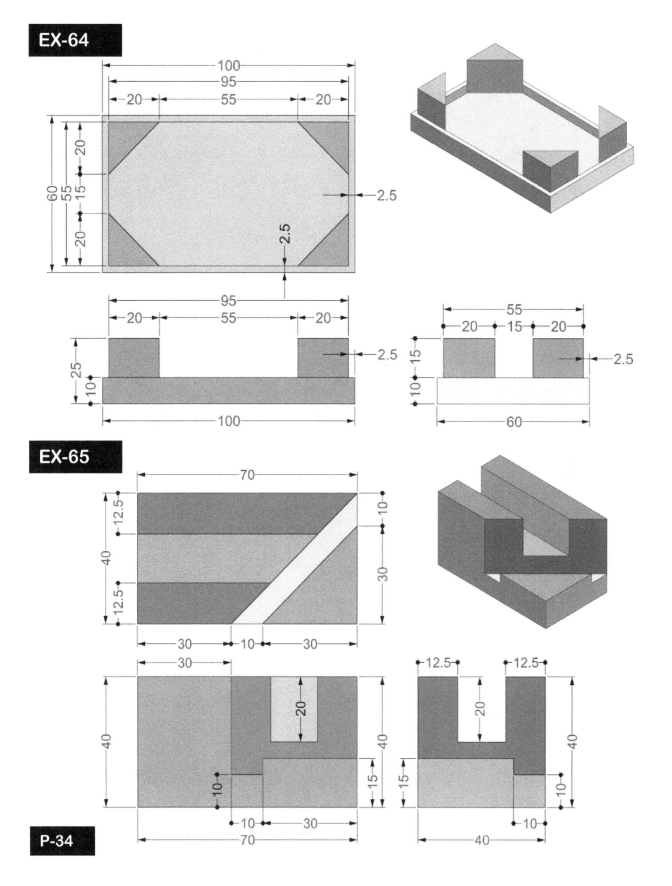

EX-64

EX-65

P-34

EX-66

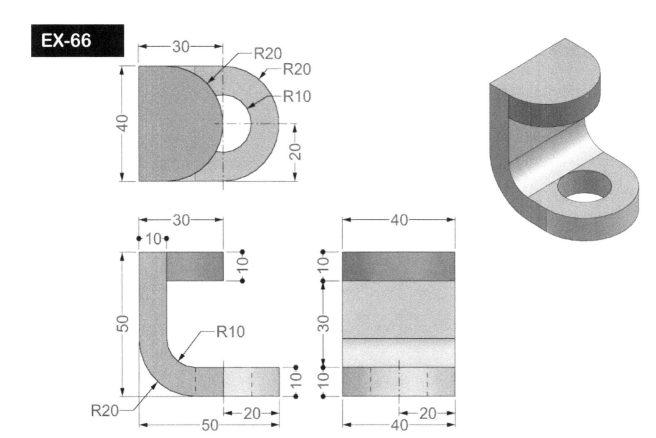

R20
R20
R10
30
40
20

30
10
10
50
R10
R20
50
20

40
10
30
10
20
40

EX-67

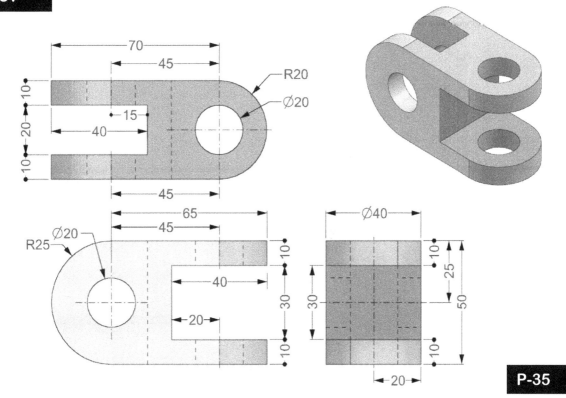

70
45
R20
Ø20
10
20
10
15
40
45

65
45
R25
Ø20
10
40
30
20
10

Ø40
10
25
30
50
10
20

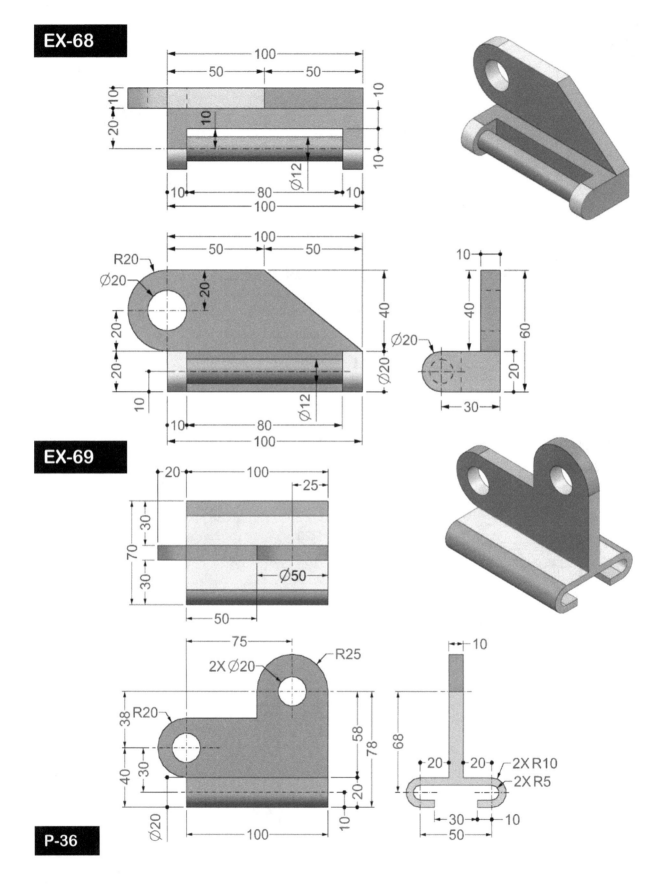

EX-68

EX-69

P-36

EX-70

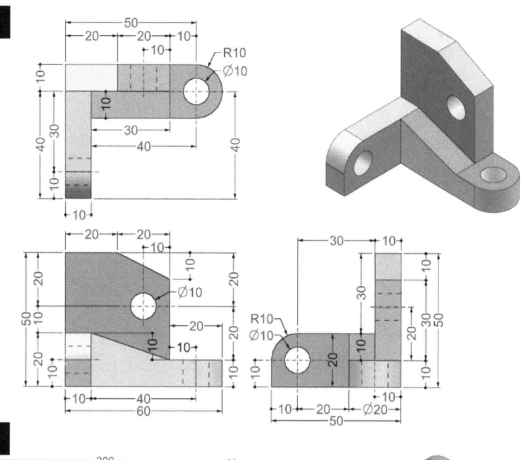

EX-71

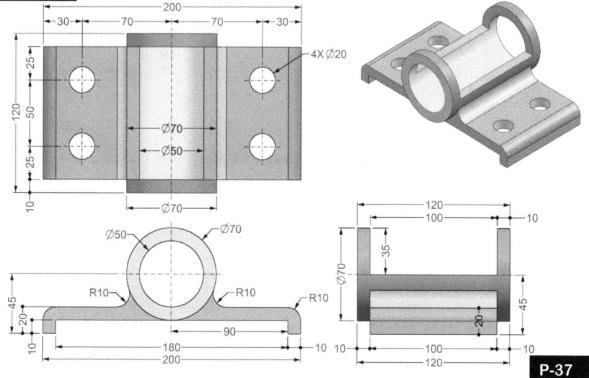

P-37

EX-72

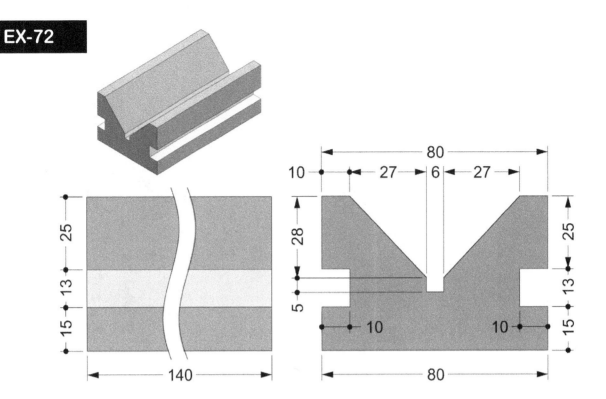

EX-73

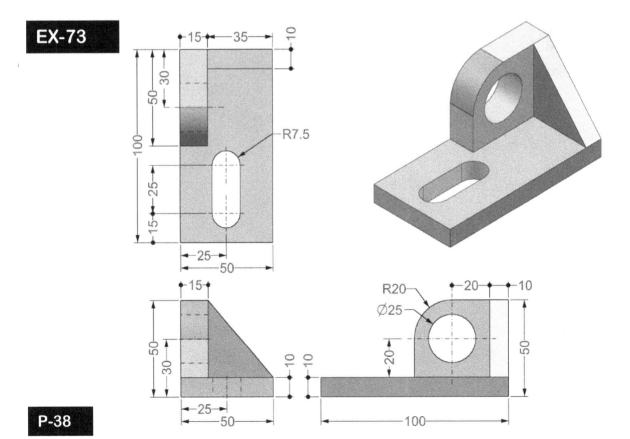

P-38

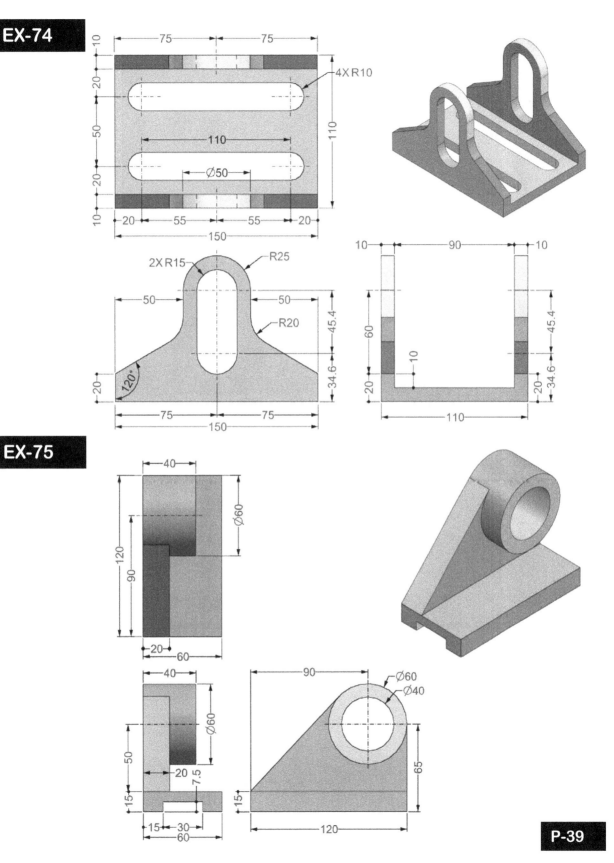

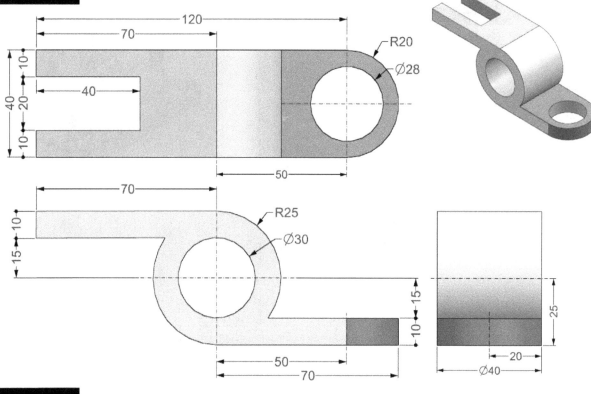

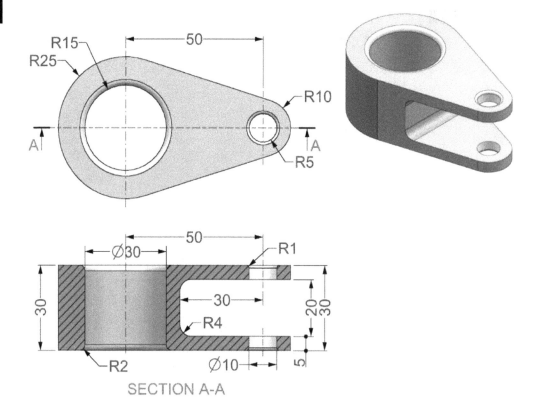

SECTION A-A

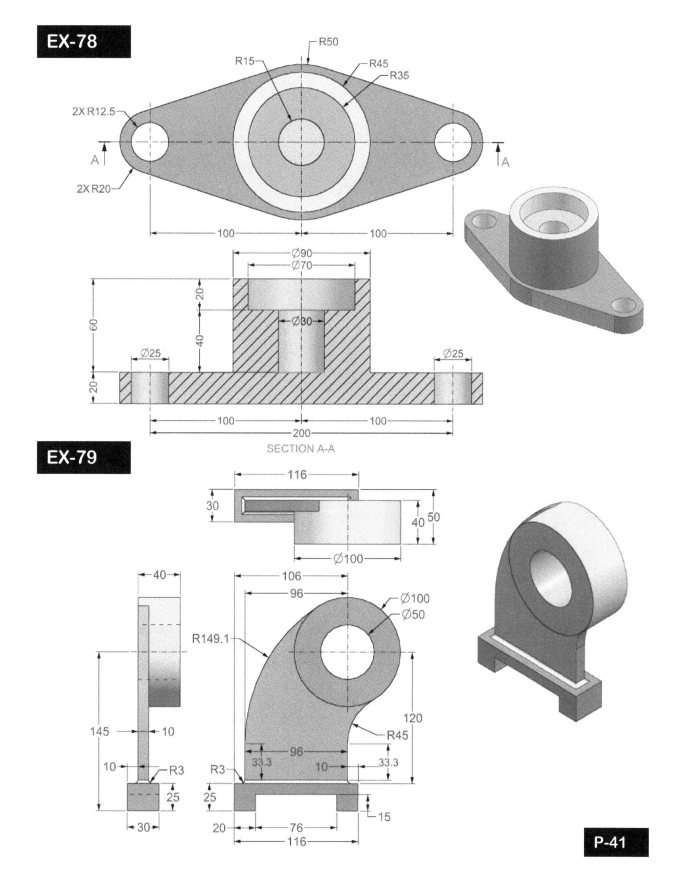

EX-78

R50
R15
R45
R35
2X R12.5
A
A
2X R20

100 — 100

Ø90
Ø70
20
60
40
Ø30
Ø25 — Ø25
20

100 — 100
200

SECTION A-A

EX-79

116
30
40 50
Ø100

40
106
96
Ø100
Ø50
R149.1
120
R45
145 — 10
145
10 — R3
R3 — 96
33.3
10 — 33.3
25
25 — 15
30
20 — 76
116

P-41

EX-80

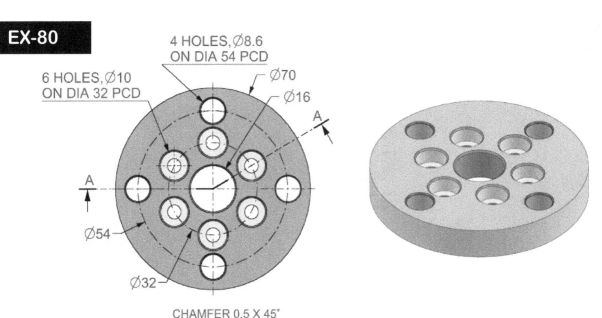

6 HOLES, ⌀10
ON DIA 32 PCD

4 HOLES, ⌀8.6
ON DIA 54 PCD

⌀70

⌀16

A

A

⌀54

⌀32

CHAMFER 0.5 X 45°

4X ⌀8.6

⌀16

6X ⌀10

10

5

5

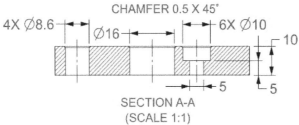

SECTION A-A
(SCALE 1:1)

EX-81

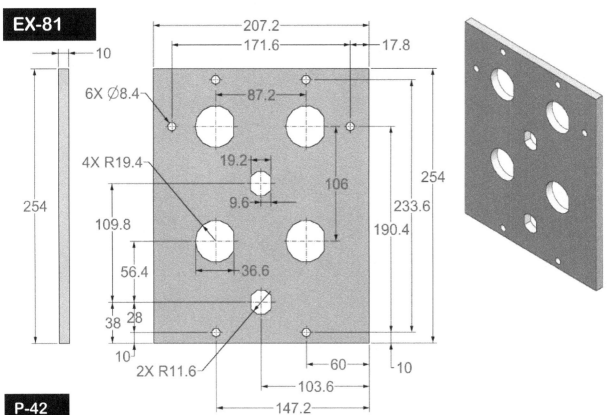

207.2

171.6

17.8

10

6X ⌀8.4

87.2

4X R19.4

19.2

9.6

254

106

233.6

190.4

254

109.8

56.4

36.6

38 28

10

2X R11.6

60

10

103.6

147.2

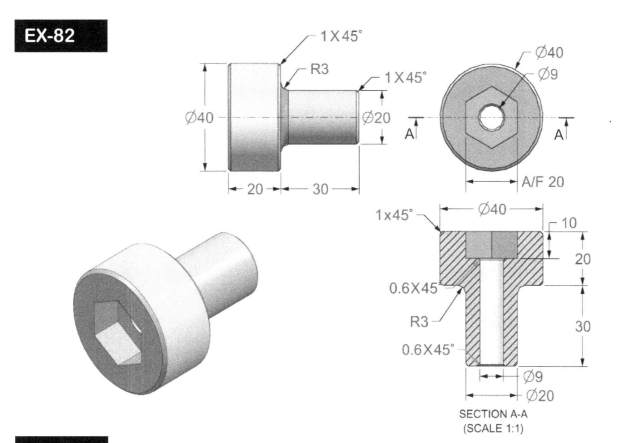

1 X 45°
R3
1 X 45°
Ø40
Ø9
Ø40
Ø20
20
30
A/F 20

1x45°
Ø40
10
20
0.6X45
R3
30
0.6X45°
Ø9
Ø20

SECTION A-A
(SCALE 1:1)

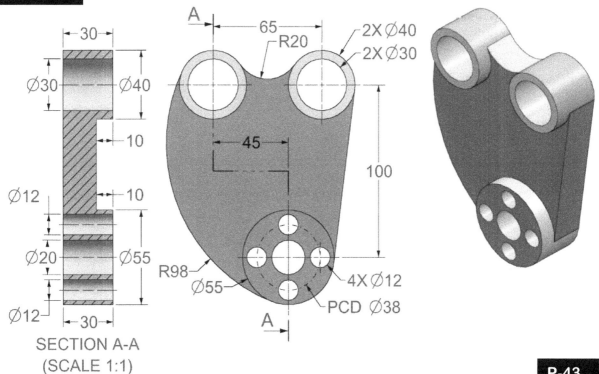

A
65
R20
2X Ø40
2X Ø30

30
Ø30
Ø40
10
10
Ø12
45
100
Ø20
Ø55
Ø12
R98
Ø55
4X Ø12
30
PCD Ø38
A

SECTION A-A
(SCALE 1:1)

EX-84

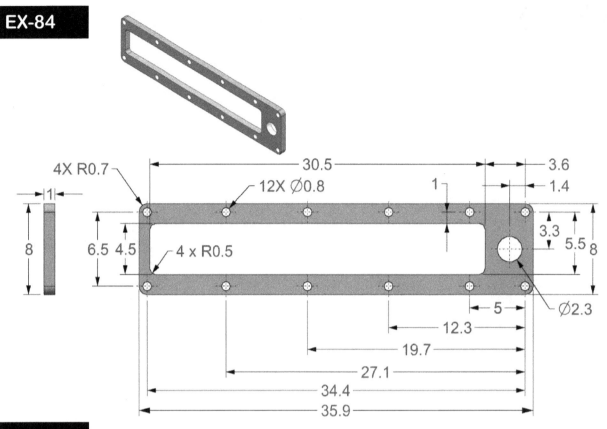

4X R0.7
12X Ø0.8
4 x R0.5
30.5
3.6
1.4
1
3.3
5.5
8
8
1
6.5 4.5
5
Ø2.3
12.3
19.7
27.1
34.4
35.9

EX-85

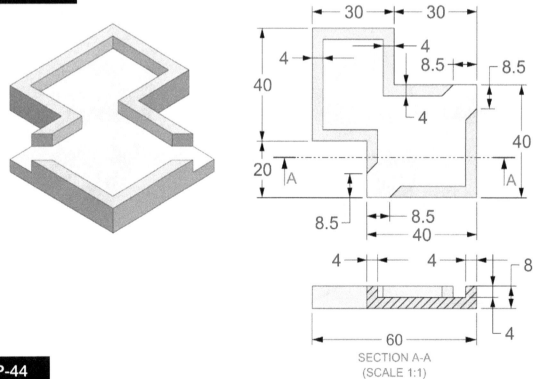

30
30
4
4
8.5
8.5
40
4
40
20
A
A
8.5
8.5
40
4
4
8
60
8.5
4

SECTION A-A
(SCALE 1:1)

P-44

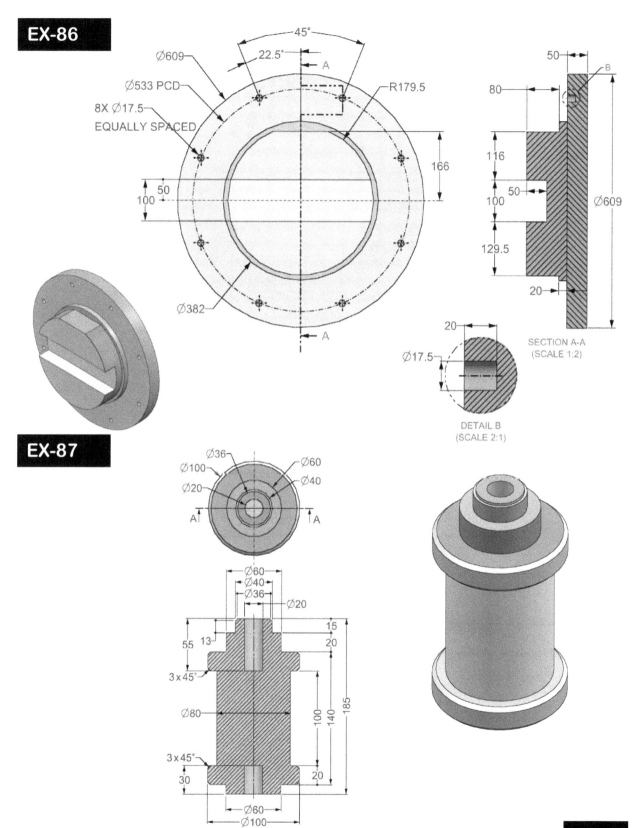

EX-86

Ø609
Ø533 PCD
8X Ø17.5
EQUALLY SPACED

45°
22.5°
A
R179.5

166
50
100

Ø382

A

50
80
B

116
50
100
129.5
20

SECTION A-A
(SCALE 1:2)

Ø609

20
Ø17.5

DETAIL B
(SCALE 2:1)

EX-87

Ø36
Ø100
Ø20
Ø60
Ø40

A
A

Ø60
Ø40
Ø36
Ø20

15
20
55
13

3 x 45°

Ø80
100
140
185

3 x 45°
30
20

Ø60
Ø100

SECTION A-A

P-45

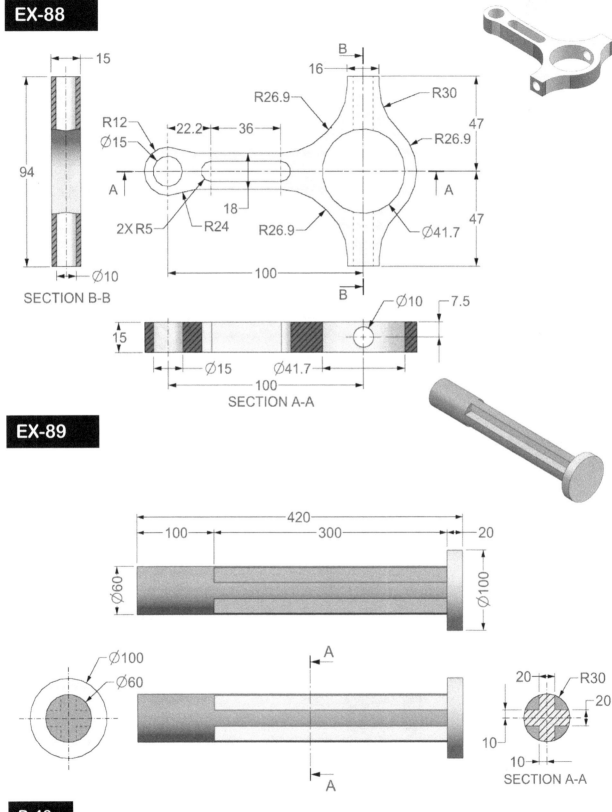

EX-88

SECTION B-B

R26.9

R30

R26.9

R12

Ø15

22.2

36

16

47

47

R24

2X R5

R26.9

R26.9

Ø41.7

18

15

94

Ø10

100

A

B

B

A

SECTION A-A

Ø10

7.5

15

Ø15

Ø41.7

100

EX-89

420

100

300

20

Ø60

Ø100

Ø100

Ø60

A

A

20

R30

20

10

10

SECTION A-A

P-46

EX-90

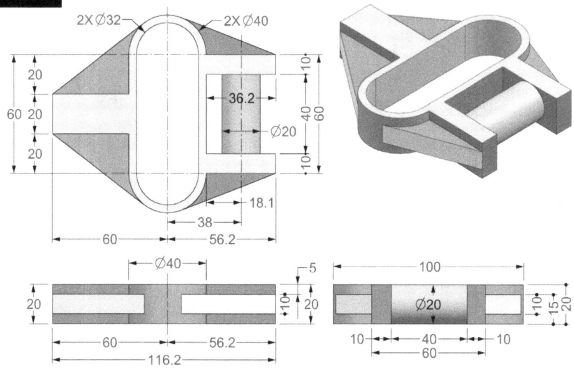

EX-91

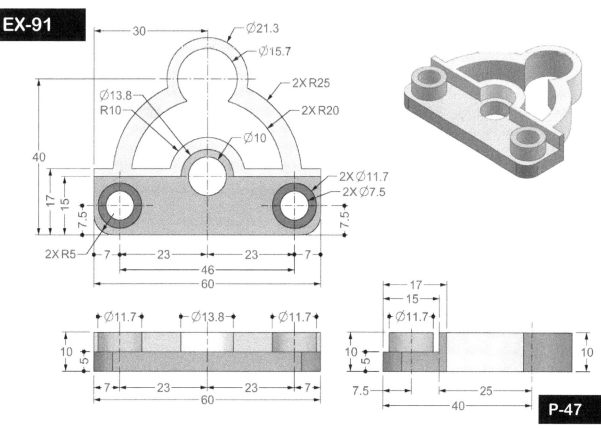

P-47

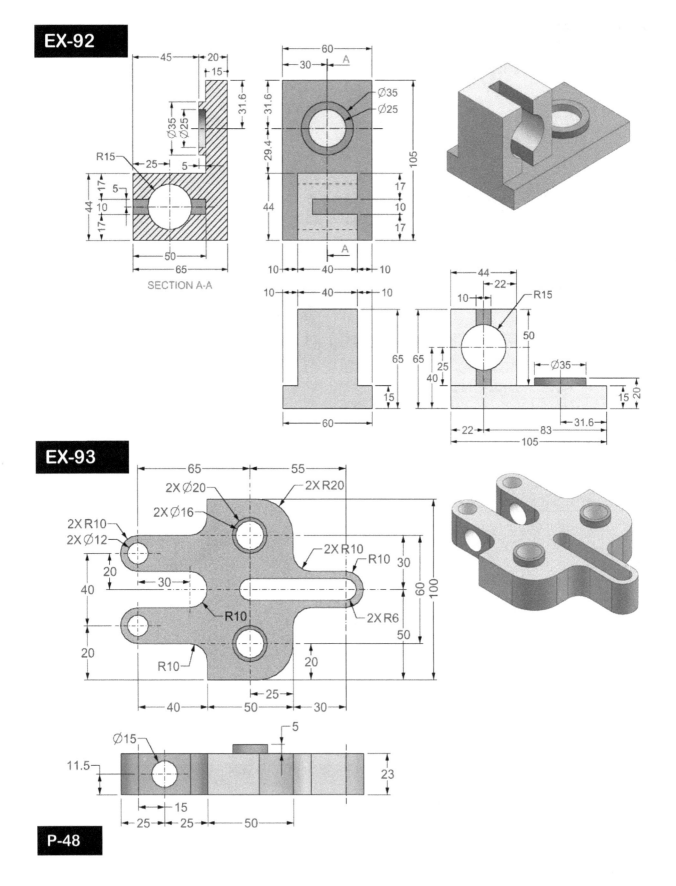

EX-92

SECTION A-A

EX-93

P-48

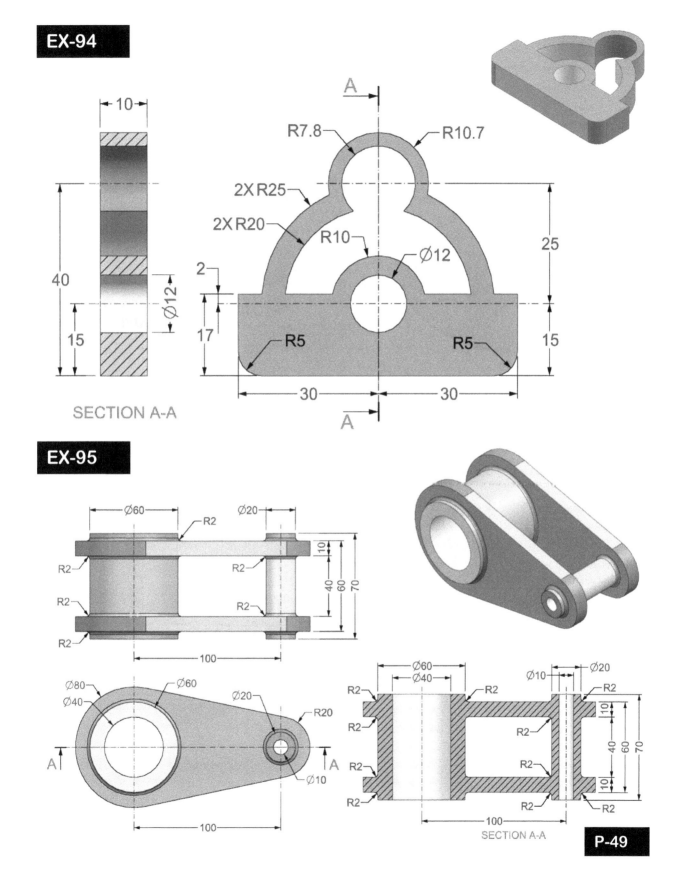

EX-94

R7.8   R10.7

2X R25

2X R20   R10   Ø12

25

10

40   Ø12

2

17   15

R5   R5

SECTION A-A

30   30

A

EX-95

Ø60   R2   Ø20

R2   R2

10

40   60   70

R2   R2

R2

100

Ø80   Ø60   Ø20   R20

Ø40

A   A

Ø10

100

Ø60   Ø20

Ø40   R2   Ø10   R2

R2   R2

10

R2   R2

40   60   70

R2   R2

10

R2   R2

100

SECTION A-A

P-49

EX-96

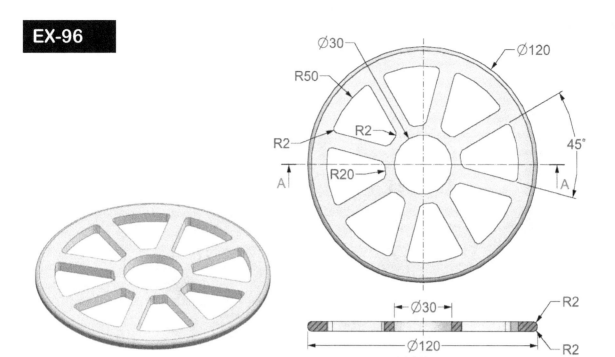

Ø30
R50
Ø120
R2
R2
R2
45°
R20

Ø30
Ø120
R2
R2
SECTION A-A

EX-97

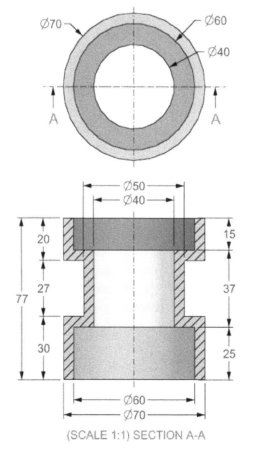
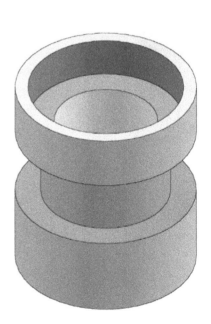

Ø70
Ø60
Ø40

A — A

Ø50
Ø40
20
15
27
37
77
30
25
Ø60
Ø70

(SCALE 1:1) SECTION A-A

P-50

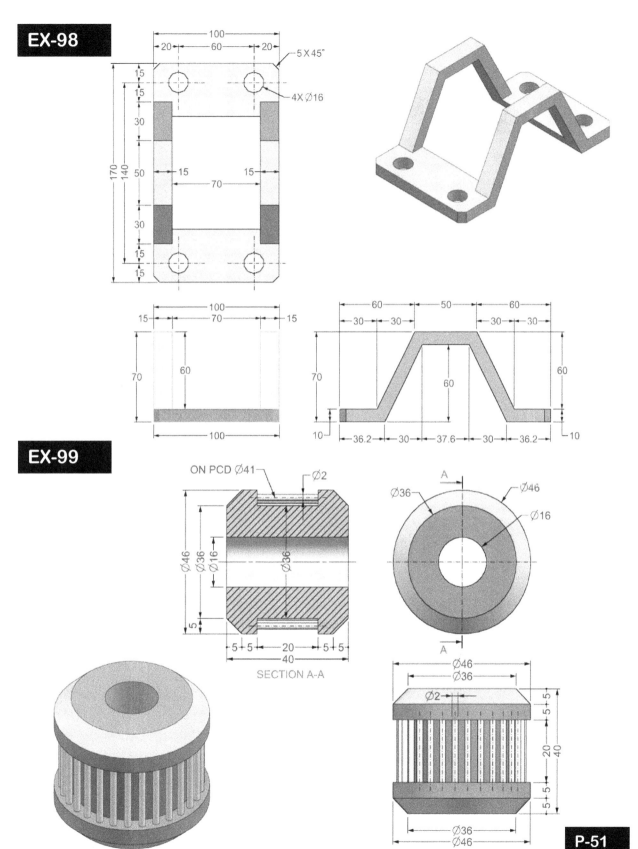

EX-98

100
20 60 20
5 X 45°
15
15
30
4X Ø16
50 15 15
70
30
15
15
170
140

100
15 70 15
70 60
100

60 50 60
30 30 30 30
70 60
10
36.2 30 37.6 30 36.2 10

EX-99

ON PCD Ø41
Ø2
Ø46
Ø36
Ø16
Ø36
5
5+5 20 5+5
40
SECTION A-A

A
Ø36
Ø46
Ø16
A

Ø46
Ø36
Ø2
5 5
20 40
5 5
Ø36
Ø46

P-51

EX-100

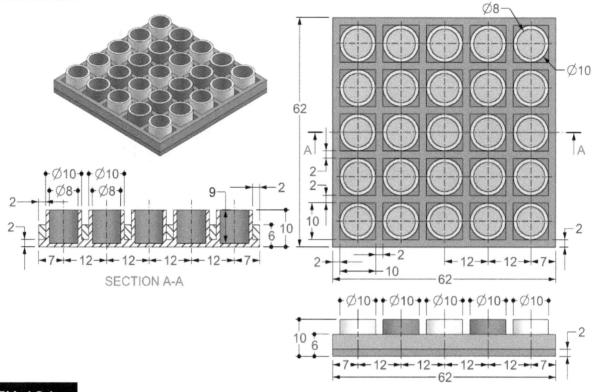

SECTION A-A

EX-101

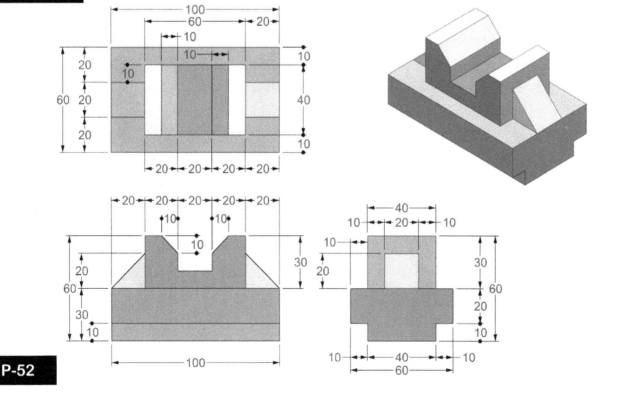

P-52

EX-102

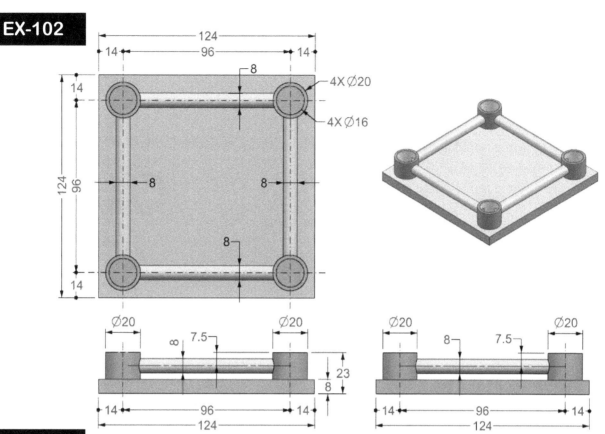

EX-103

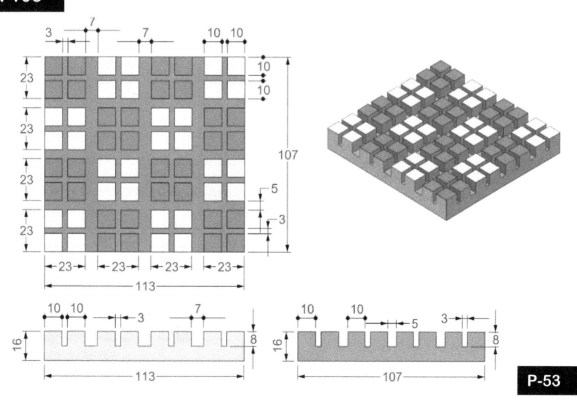

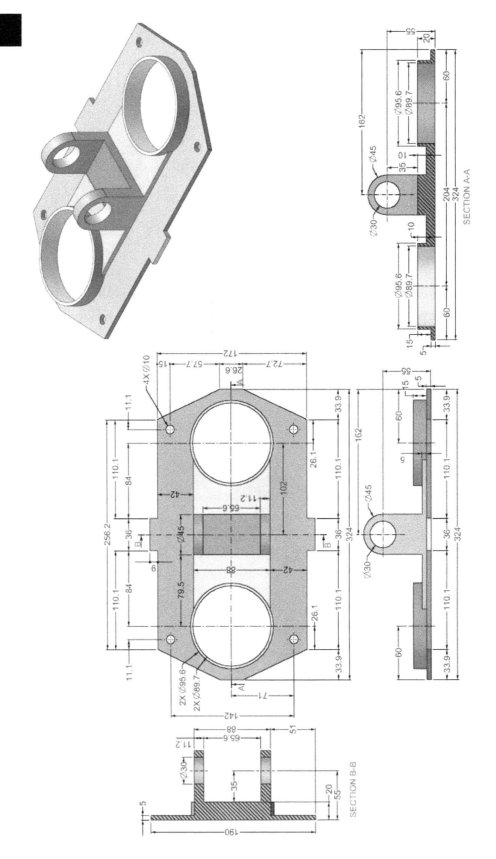

SECTION A-A

SECTION B-B

EX-105

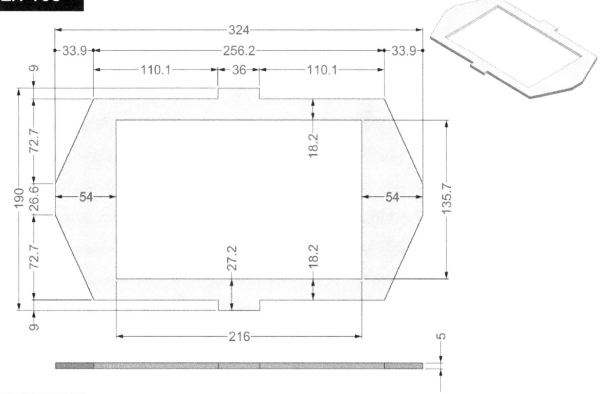

EX-106

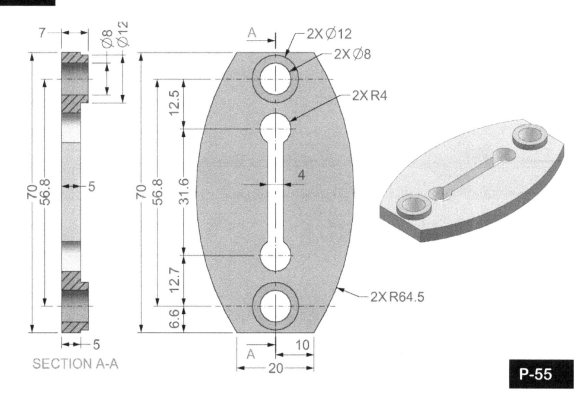

SECTION A-A

EX-107

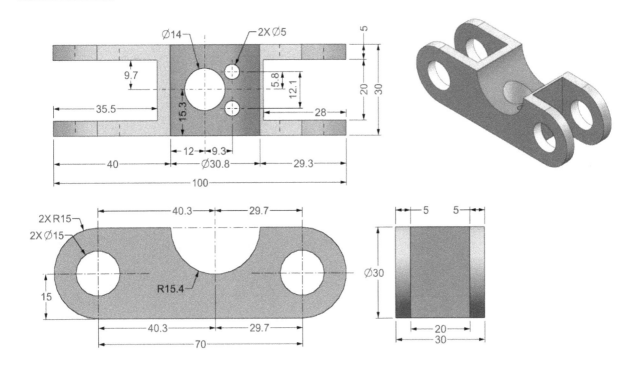

EX-108

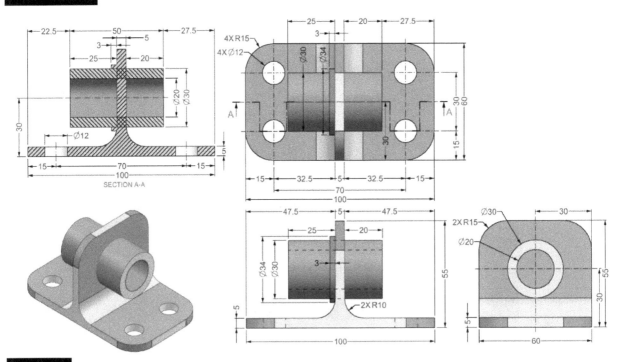

P-56

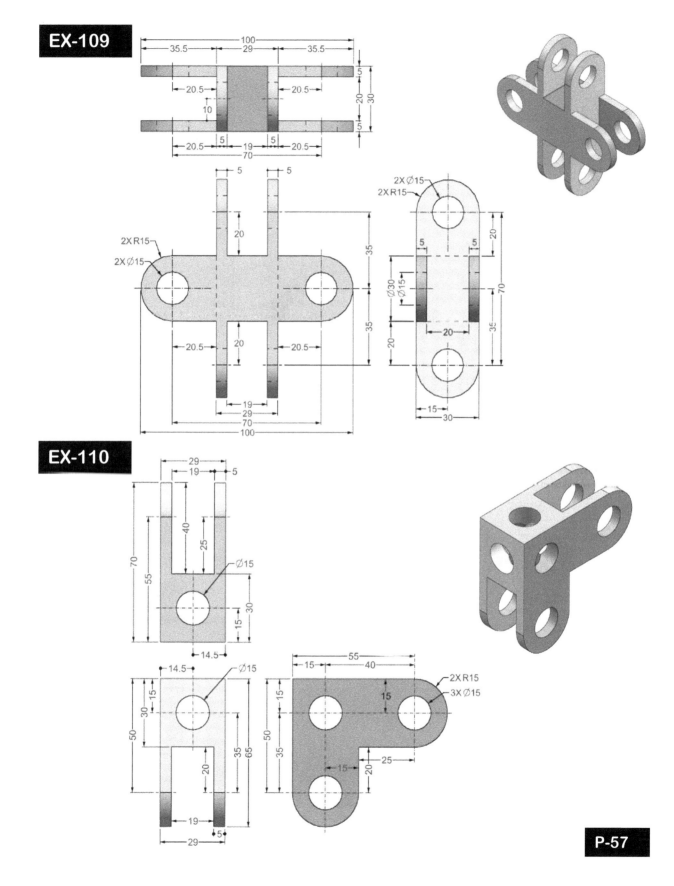

EX-109

EX-110

P-57

EX-111

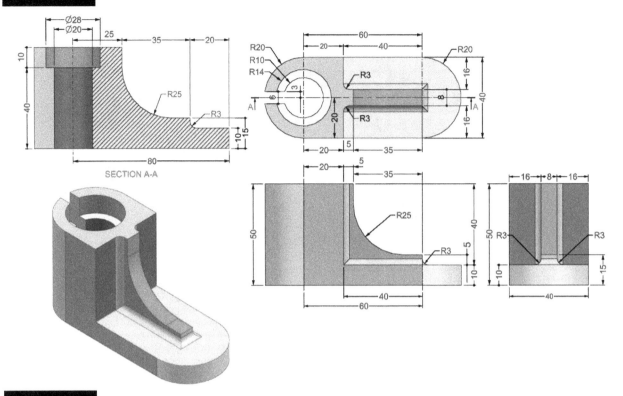

Ø28
Ø20
25
35
20
R20
R10
R14
R3
R20
10
40
R25
R3
16
40
16
80
SECTION A-A
20
5
35
R3
R3
20
5

20
5
35
R25
50
40
5
R3
60
40
16 8 16
R3
R3
50
10
15
40

EX-112

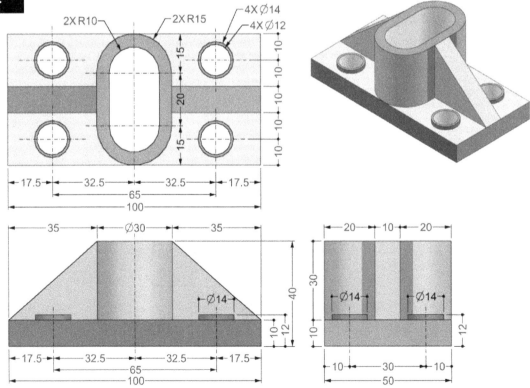

2X R10
2X R15
4X Ø14
4X Ø12
15
10
10
10
10
20
15
10
17.5
32.5
32.5
17.5
65
100

35
Ø30
35
20
10
20
Ø14
40
30
Ø14
Ø14
10
12
10
17.5
32.5
32.5
17.5
65
100
10
30
10
50

P-58

EX-113

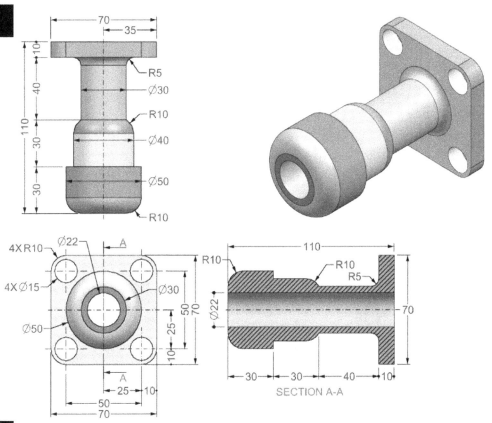

SECTION A-A

EX-114

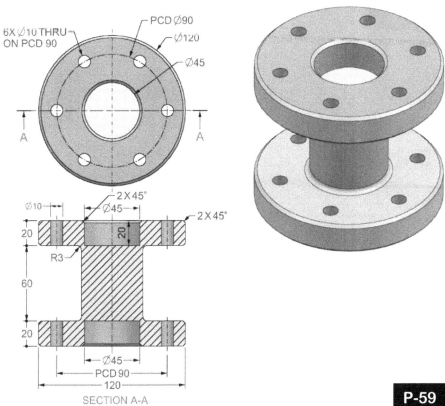

SECTION A-A

Ø120
6X Ø10
6X Ø8
PCD Ø90
Ø68
Ø45

Ø120
Ø68
R2
Ø10
10
10
20
120
60
20
10
PCD 90

Ø120
PCD 90
Ø68
Ø45
Ø10
20
40
60
20
R3
R3
2 X 45°
Ø8
Ø55
Ø50
20
Ø45
Ø8

SECTION A-A

120
100
10
25
50
25
10
4X Ø10
4X R5
25
25
A
A
30
50
15
10
Ø30
Ø20

20
80
50
45
20
R5
120

80
20
70
25
Ø10
30
R5
10
100
120

SECTION A-A

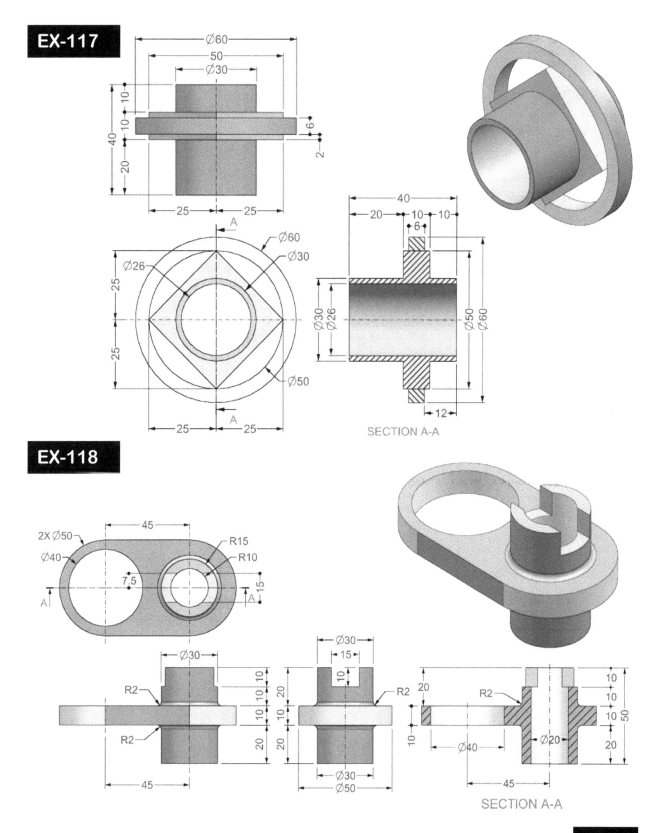

EX-117

SECTION A-A

EX-118

SECTION A-A

P-61

EX-119

Ø190
Ø55

2X R20
Ø140
70
2X R25

25
50

Ø55
Ø75
Ø100
Ø180
Ø190

SECTION A-A

A

R25

25
50

Ø75
Ø190

A

Ø75
Ø190
Ø55
Ø180
Ø100

EX-120

Ø50
Ø60
10
20
15
20
20
20
40
20
20
45
15
100

R15
A
Ø50
Ø70
Ø70
Ø40
A
Ø20
Ø30
Ø60
100
100

Ø50
Ø30
Ø60
Ø40
10
90
20
15
20
20
40
Ø20
15
20
45
100
100

SECTION A-A

P-62

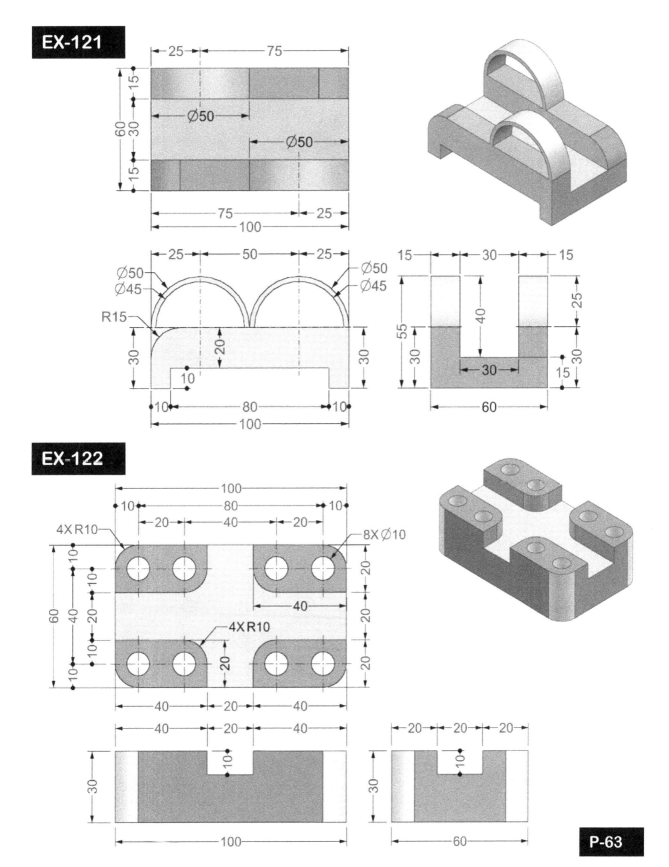

EX-121

EX-122

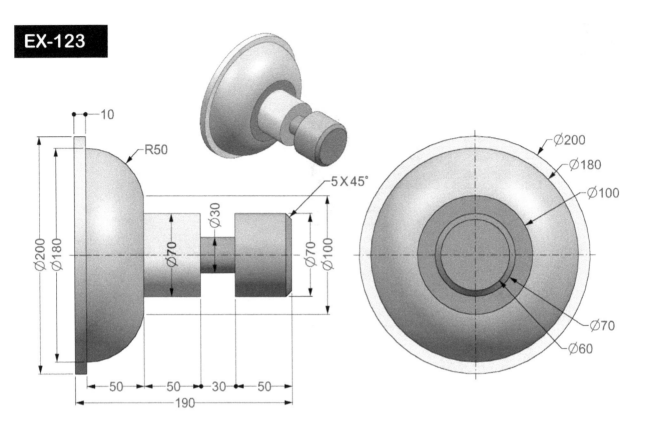

10
R50
5 X 45°
Ø30
Ø70
Ø70
Ø100
Ø200
Ø180
50 50 30 50
190

Ø200
Ø180
Ø100
Ø70
Ø60

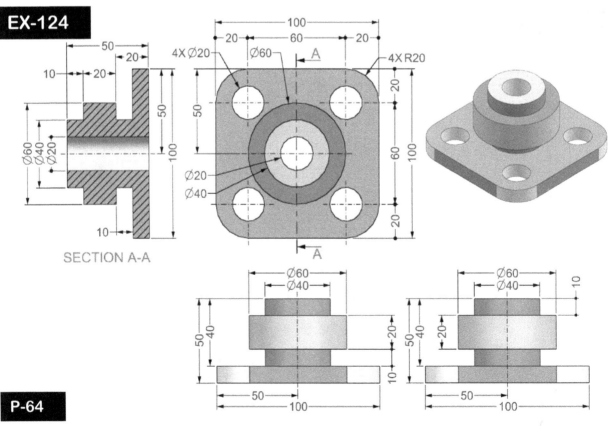

50
10 20 20
4X Ø20
Ø60
100
20
60
20
A
4X R20
50
60
100
20
Ø60
Ø40
Ø20
Ø20
Ø40
10
A
SECTION A-A

Ø60
Ø40
50 40
20
50
Ø60
Ø40
10
50 40
20
50 50
100 100

EX-125

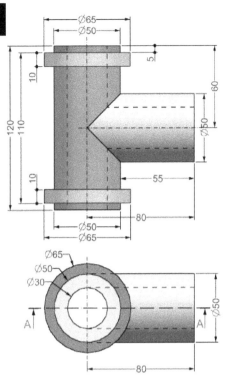

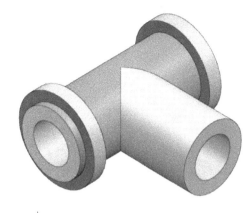

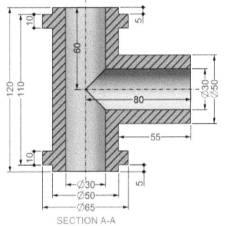

SECTION A-A

EX-126

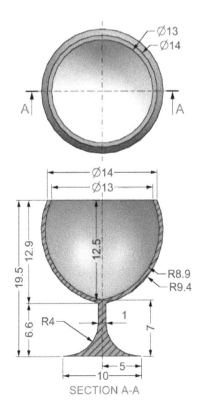

SECTION A-A

P-65

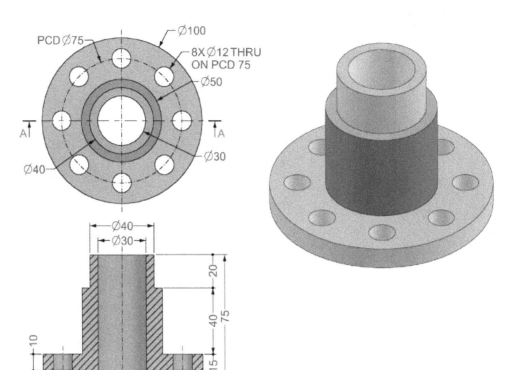

PCD Ø75
Ø100
8X Ø12 THRU
ON PCD 75
Ø50
Ø30
Ø40

A | A

Ø40
Ø30
20
75
40
10
15
Ø50
75
Ø100

SECTION A-A

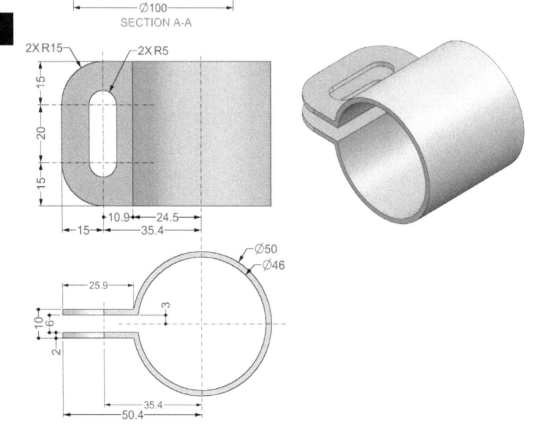

2X R15
2X R5
15
20
15
10.9
24.5
15
35.4

Ø50
Ø46
25.9
3
10
6
2
35.4
50.4

EX-129

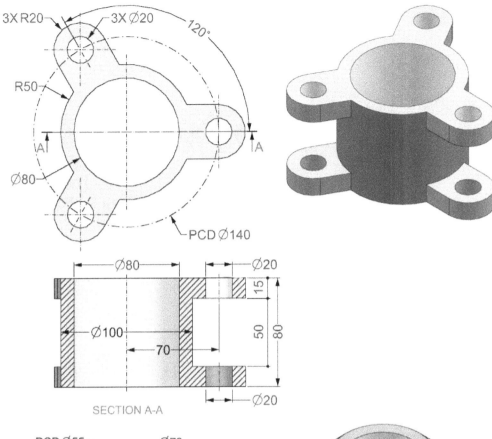

3X R20 3X Ø20 120°

R50

Ø80

PCD Ø140

Ø80 Ø20

Ø100

70

15

50

80

Ø20

SECTION A-A

EX-130

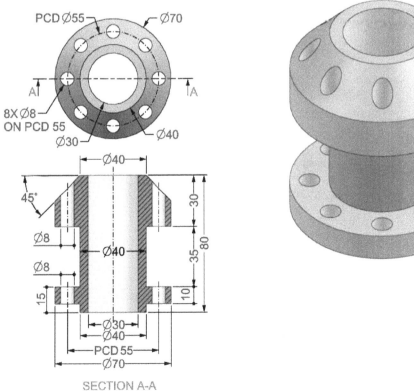

PCD Ø55 Ø70

8X Ø8
ON PCD 55

Ø30 Ø40

A A

Ø40

45°

Ø8

Ø40

Ø8

15

30

35

80

10

Ø30
Ø40
PCD 55
Ø70

SECTION A-A

EX-131

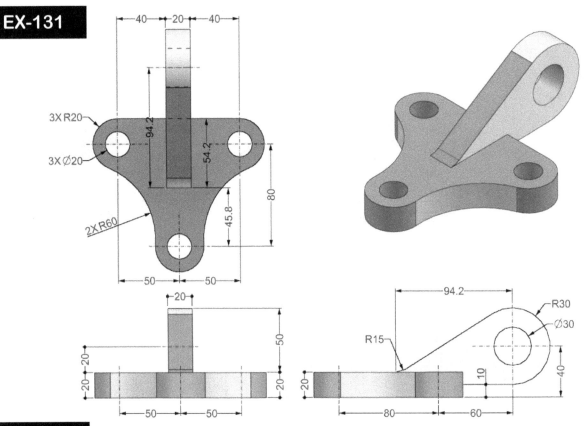

EX-132

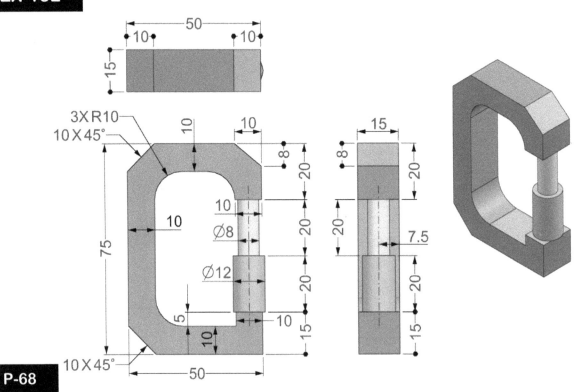

EX-133

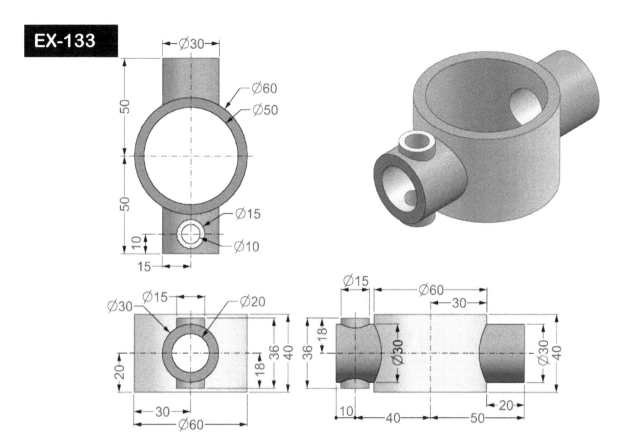

EX-134

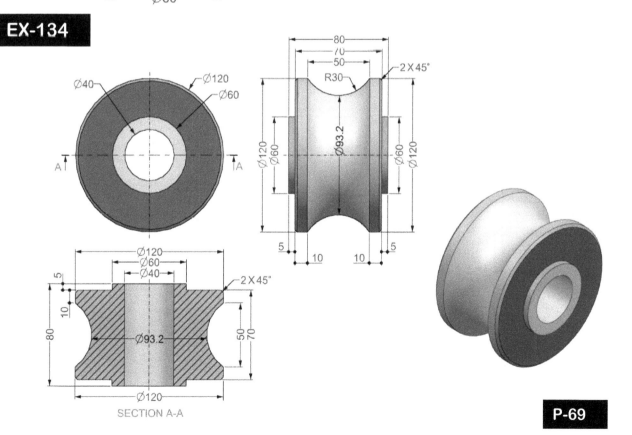

SECTION A-A

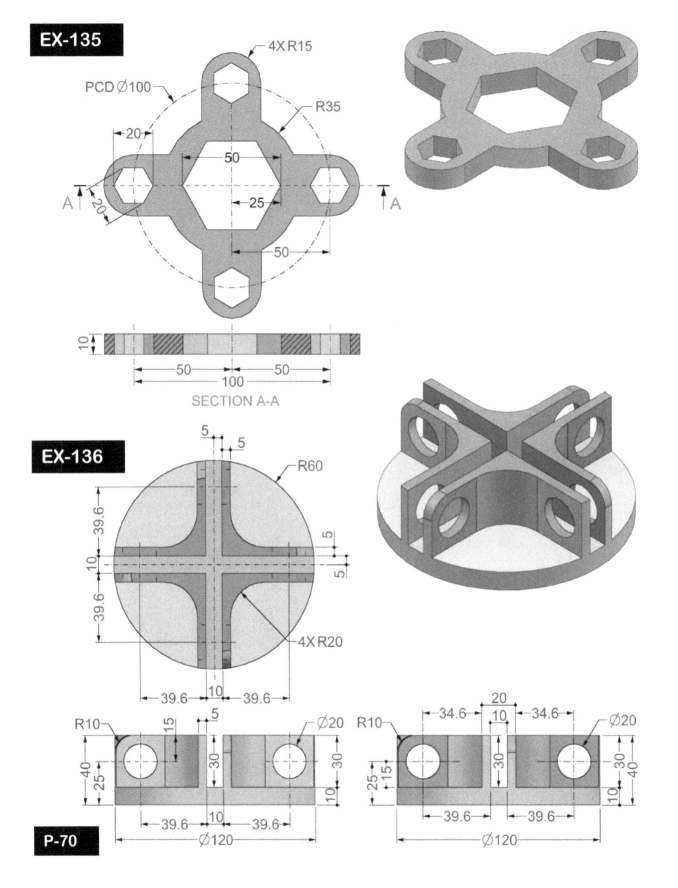

EX-135

4X R15

PCD ⌀100

R35

20

50

25

50

20

A — A

SECTION A-A

50
100
50

10

EX-136

5
5

R60

39.6

39.6

10

5
5

4X R20

39.6 — 10 — 39.6

R10

15
5

⌀20

40
25

30
30

10

39.6 — 10 — 39.6

⌀120

R10

20
34.6 — 10 — 34.6

⌀20

40
25
15

30
30

10

39.6 — 39.6

⌀120

P-70

EX-137

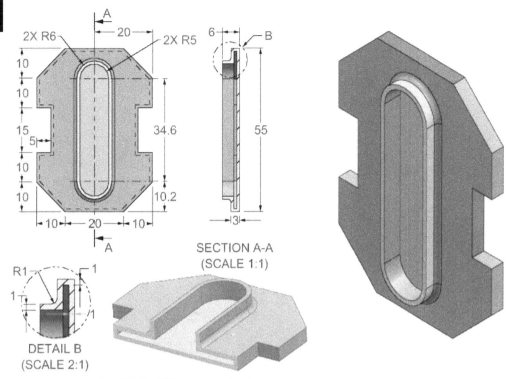

2X R6
20
2X R5
6
B
A
10
10
15
5
34.6
55
10
10
10
10.2
10
20
10
3
A

SECTION A-A
(SCALE 1:1)

R1
1
1
1
1

DETAIL B
(SCALE 2:1)

SHELL THICKNESS = 1MM
ALL INSIDE WALL THICKNESS

EX-138

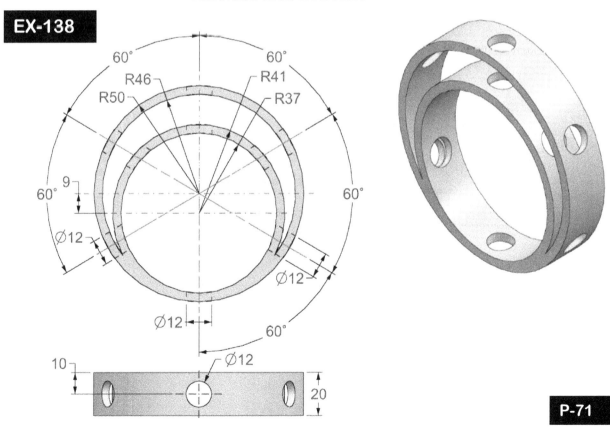

60°
60°
R46
R41
R50
R37
60°
9
60°
Ø12
Ø12
Ø12
60°

10
Ø12
20

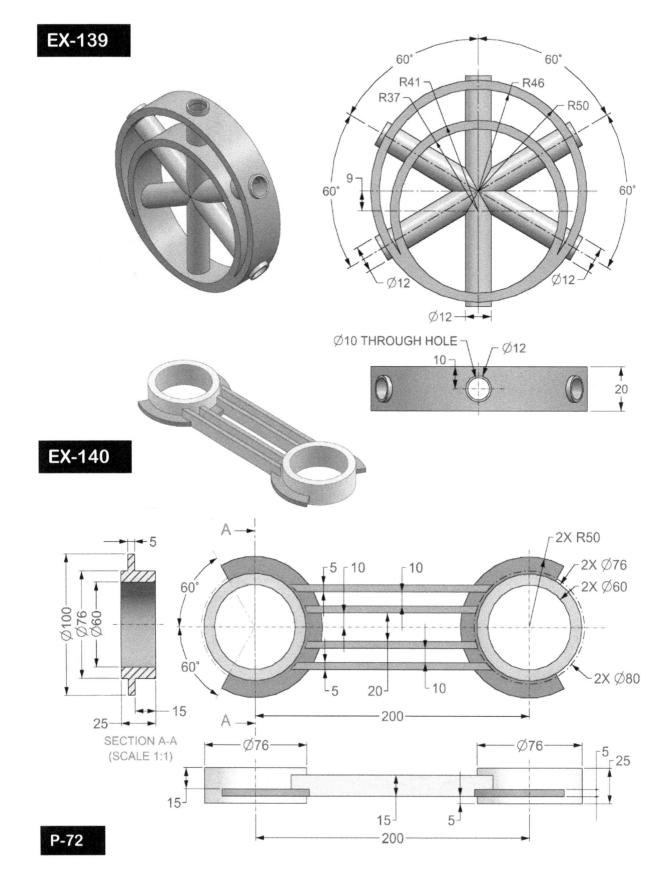

EX-139

R41
R46
R37
R50
60° 60°
60° 60°
60° 60°
9
Ø12
Ø12
Ø12

Ø10 THROUGH HOLE
Ø12
10
20

EX-140

5
60°
60°
Ø100
Ø76
Ø60
15
25

A
A

5 10 10
5
20 10
5

2X R50
2X Ø76
2X Ø60
2X Ø80

200

SECTION A-A
(SCALE 1:1)

Ø76
Ø76
5
25
15
15 5
200

P-72

EX-141

Ø100
Ø60
Ø6
Ø120

Ø60
Ø6
30
R5
R40.7
10
10
100
Ø60
50
R5
20
Ø80
R2
R5
30
Ø120

EX-142

18
14
15
41.4
15.4
R15
R10
46.8
Ø16.2
Ø8
8
Ø20.4
23.4
26
Ø16.2
R6

15
10 20
5

P-73

EX-143

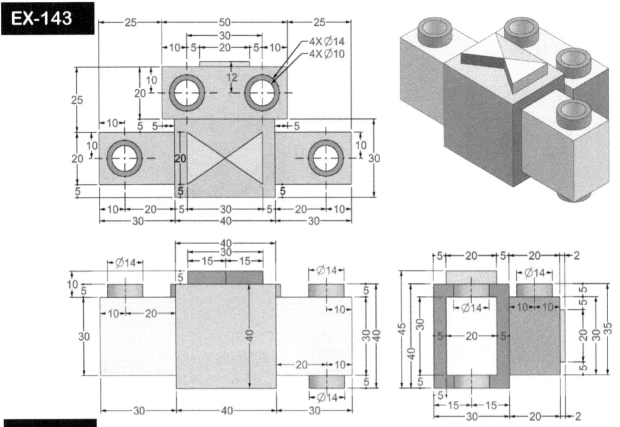

EX-144

8X Ø26 THRU HOLE
ON PCD 160

PCD Ø160
Ø80
Ø60

SECTION A-A

8X Ø12

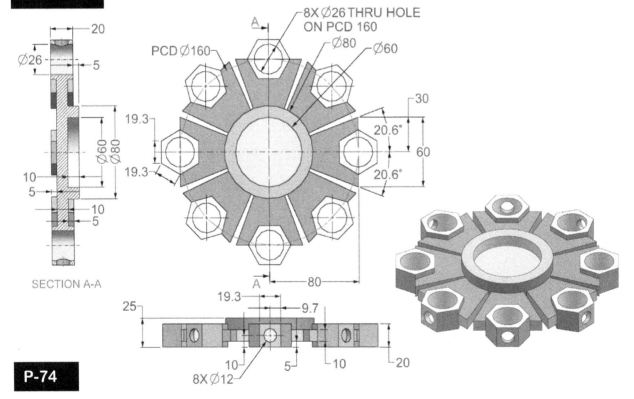

P-74

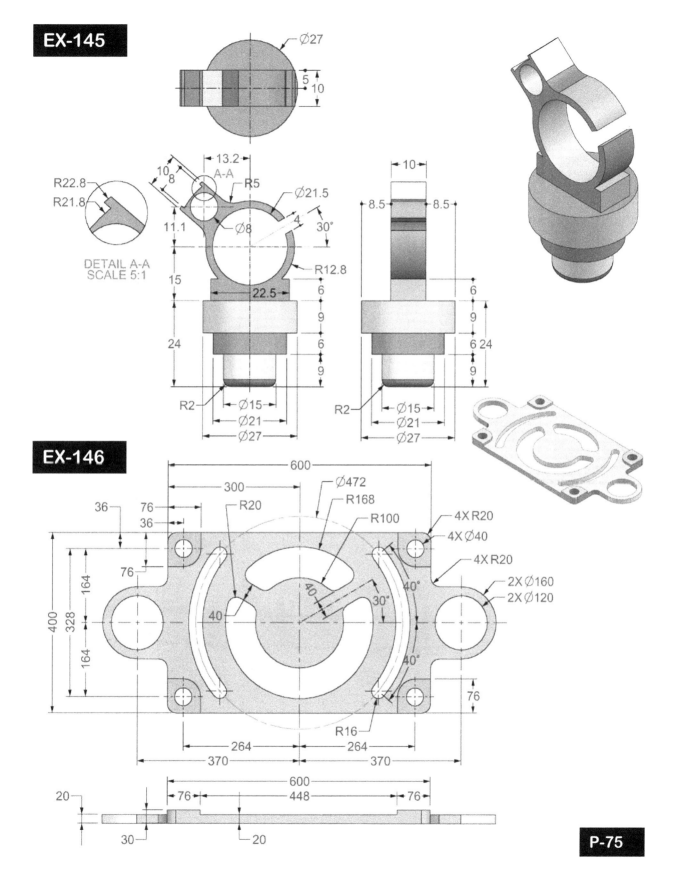

EX-145

⌀27

5
10

R22.8
R21.8

DETAIL A-A
SCALE 5:1

13.2
10
8
A-A
R5
⌀21.5
11.1
⌀8
4
30°
15
R12.8
22.5
24
6
9
6
9
R2
⌀15
⌀21
⌀27

10
8.5   8.5
6
9
6 24
9
R2
⌀15
⌀21
⌀27

EX-146

600
300
⌀472
R168
R100
36
76
R20
4X R20
36
4X ⌀40
76
4X R20
164
2X ⌀160
400
328
40
2X ⌀120
40°
164
40
30°
40°
264
264
76
R16
370
370

600
76   448   76
20
20
30

P-75

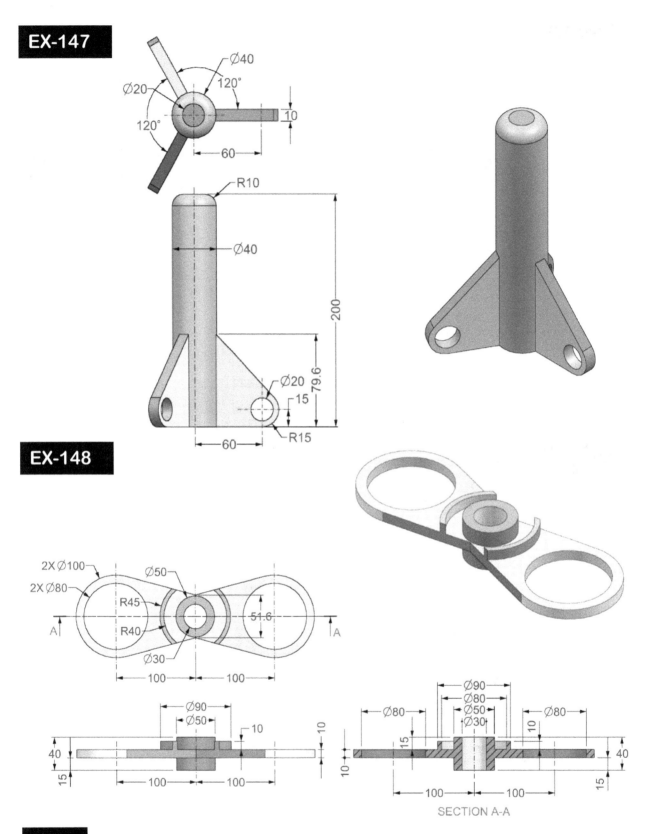

EX-147

Ø20
120°
120°
Ø40
120°
10
60

R10
Ø40
200
79.6
Ø20
15
60
R15

EX-148

2X Ø100
2X Ø80
Ø50
R45
R40
Ø30
A
51.6
A
100
100

Ø90
Ø50
10
10
40
15
100
100

Ø90
Ø80
Ø50
Ø30
Ø80
Ø80
15
10
10
10
40
15
100
100

SECTION A-A

P-76

EX-149

2X R5 — R24 — R30 — Ø41.7

Ø24

18

A

Ø15

2X R5

22.2 — 35.9

R26.9

100

100

15

5

Ø15

5

Ø24

Ø41.7

SECTION A-A

EX-150

67.5

17.8

R16.7 — R21.5

R9.6 — R4

13.3 14.4 10

R15.7

Ø12

R6.1

R6.2

2X R19.2

45.9 — 3.6 — 19

5

Ø12

SECTION A-A

EX-151

Ø8
6.5
10
28
R1.5
R1.5
11
27
Ø10
B-B
SECTION A-A

Ø20
A
R3
35
15°
20
5
A
Ø13.3
Ø16

R8
R6.7
R10
R4
R5

DETAIL B-B
SCALE 5:1
1
45°

EX-152

Ø20
Ø36
Ø58
Ø52
Ø16

Ø36
Ø20
R8
8
2
135°
Ø16
R11.2
76
21.6
13
R6
Ø16
R3
20
13.5
15.8
10.7
10

SECTION A-A

A
58
3
R3
R2
Ø52
76
R6
A
40

P-78

EX-153

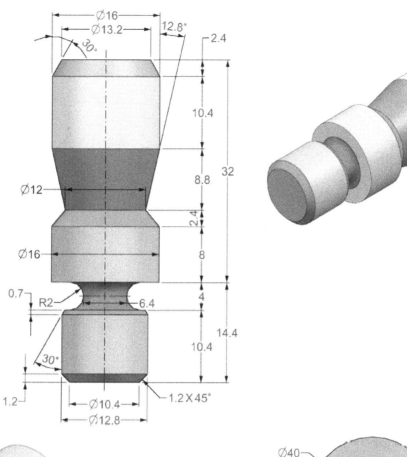

Ø16
Ø13.2
12.8°
30°
2.4
10.4
32
8.8
Ø12
2.4
Ø16
8
0.7
R2
6.4
4
14.4
10.4
30°
1.2
Ø10.4
Ø12.8
1.2 X 45°

EX-154

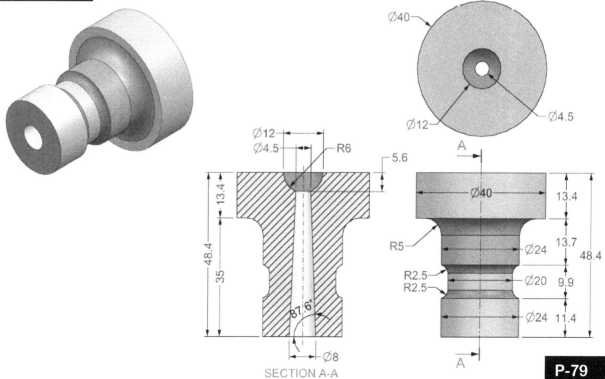

Ø40
Ø12
Ø4.5
A
Ø12
Ø4.5
R6
5.6
13.4
48.4
35
87.6°
Ø8
SECTION A-A

Ø40
R5
13.4
13.7
R2.5
Ø24
Ø20
48.4
R2.5
9.9
Ø24
11.4
A

P-79

EX-155

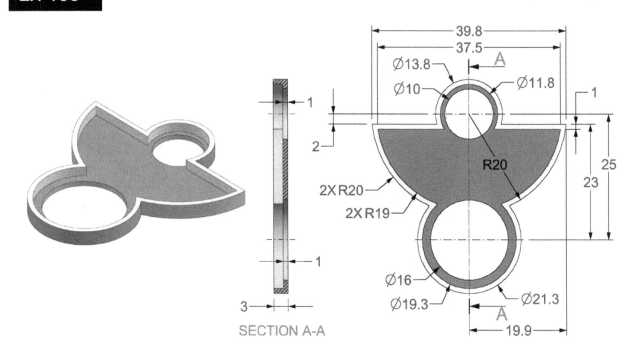

Ø13.8
Ø10
Ø11.8
39.8
37.5
A
R20
25
23
2X R20
2X R19
Ø16
Ø19.3
Ø21.3
19.9

1
2
1
3

SECTION A-A

EX-156

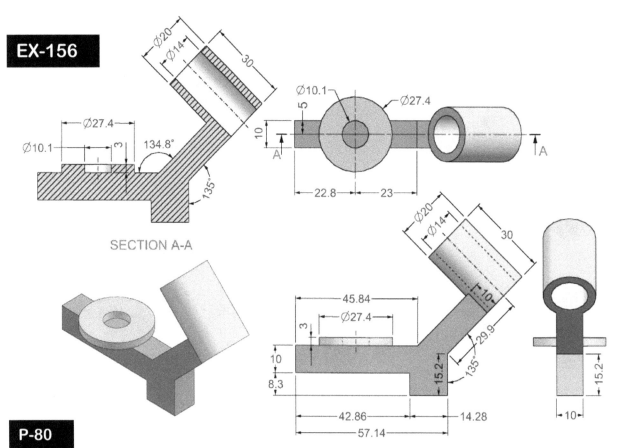

Ø20
Ø14
30
Ø27.4
Ø10.1
3
134.8°
135°

SECTION A-A

Ø10.1
Ø27.4
5
10
A
A
22.8
23

Ø20
Ø14
30
10
45.84
Ø27.4
3
29.9
135°
15.2
10
8.3
42.86
14.28
57.14
15.2
10

P-80

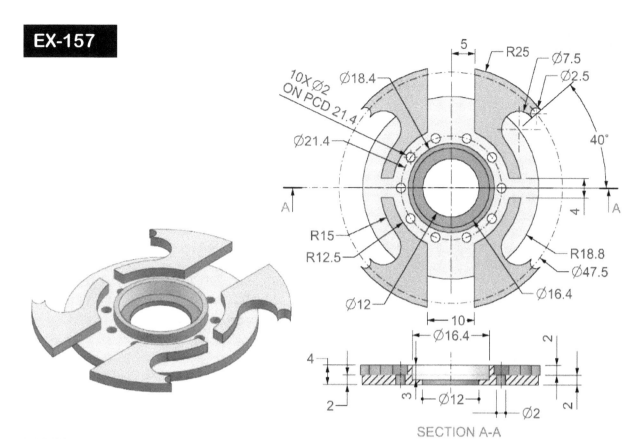

SECTION A-A

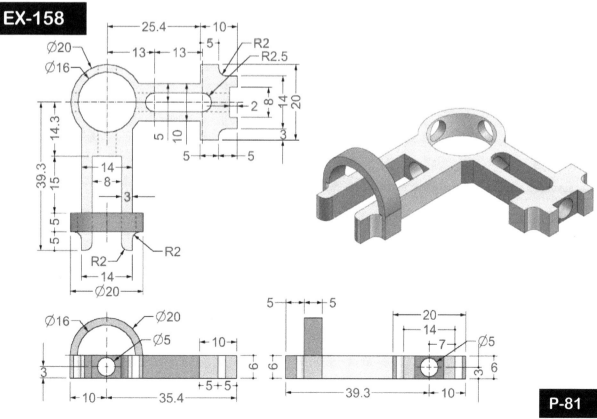

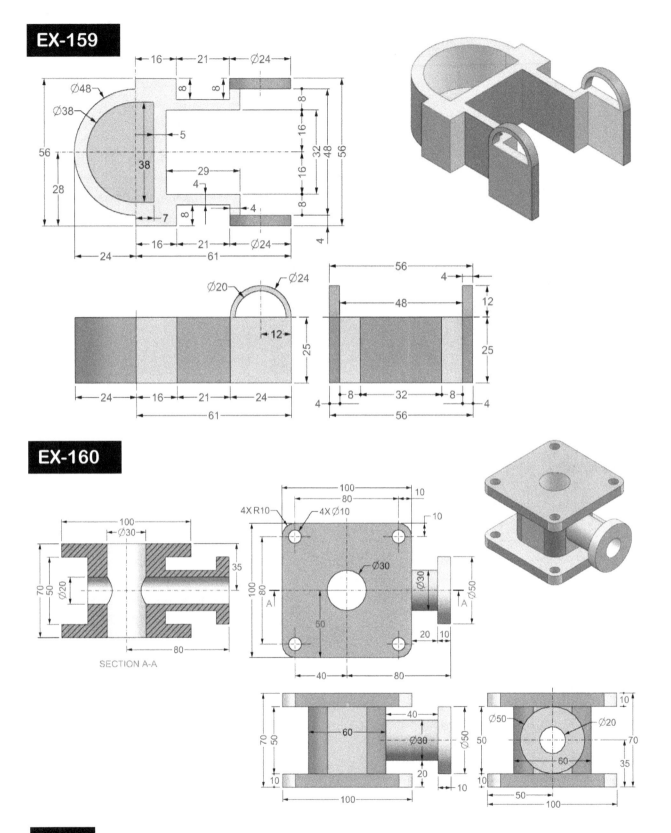

EX-159

EX-160

SECTION A-A

4X R10
4X Ø10

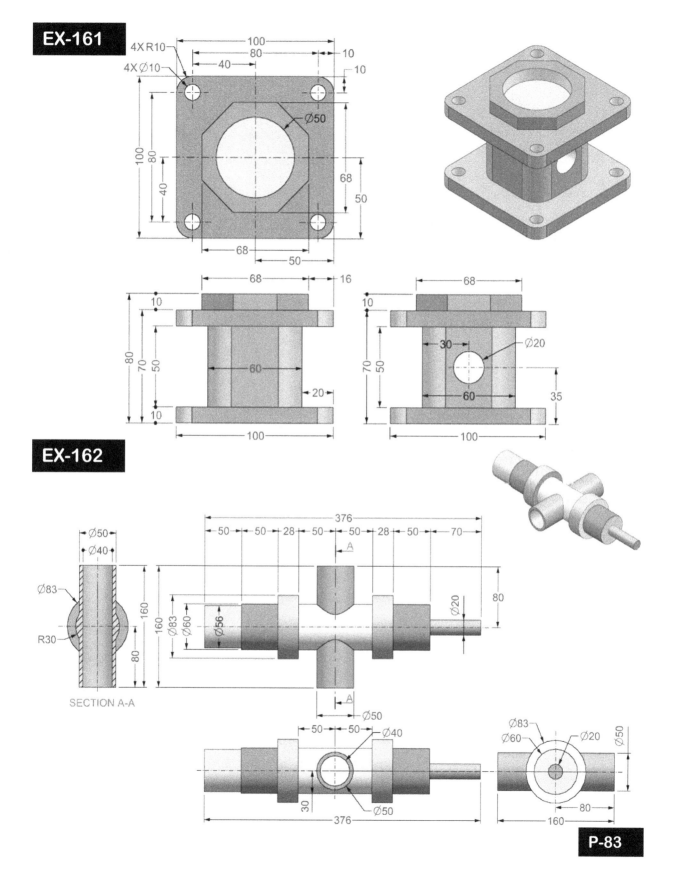

EX-161

4X R10
4X Ø10
100
80
40
10
10
100
80
40
68
50
Ø50
50
68
50

68
16
10
80
70
50
10
60
20
100

68
10
70
50
30
Ø20
60
100
35

EX-162

Ø50
Ø40
Ø83
R30
160
80
SECTION A-A

376
50 50 28 50 50 28 50 70
A
160
Ø83
Ø60
Ø56
Ø20
80
A
Ø50

50 50
Ø40
30
Ø50
376

Ø83
Ø60
Ø20
Ø50
80
160

P-83

EX-163

PCD ⌀160
4X ⌀20
R100
2X ⌀20
2X R10
⌀40
⌀20
⌀20
PCD ⌀80.5
2X ⌀14 THRU HOLES
⌀120

TOP VIEW

⌀20
⌀20
20
10
⌀20
SECTION A-A

10
20
⌀10
SECTION B-B

⌀20
⌀40
BOTTOM VIEW

10
⌀20
⌀20
⌀20
20
SECTION C-C

EX-164

68
28.2
4X R10
4X ⌀10
10
⌀50
⌀30
68
28.2
80
100
A
40
A
10
10
40
40
10
80
100

16
68
16
⌀18
80
70
50
25
30
60
10
35
50
100

100
68
⌀50
10
⌀18
10 10
50
25
⌀30
50
50
100
SECTION A-A

P-84

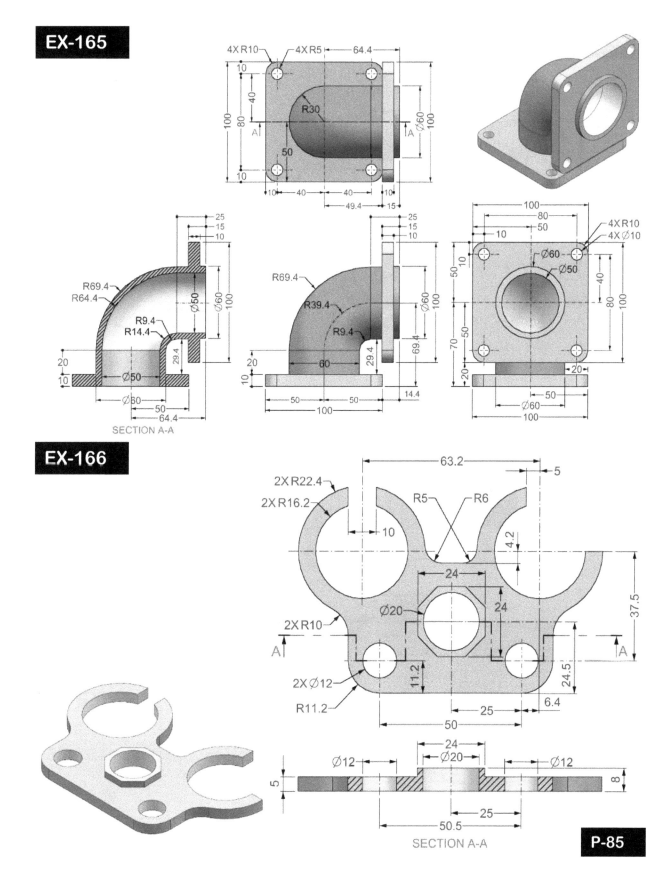

EX-165

SECTION A-A

EX-166

SECTION A-A

P-85

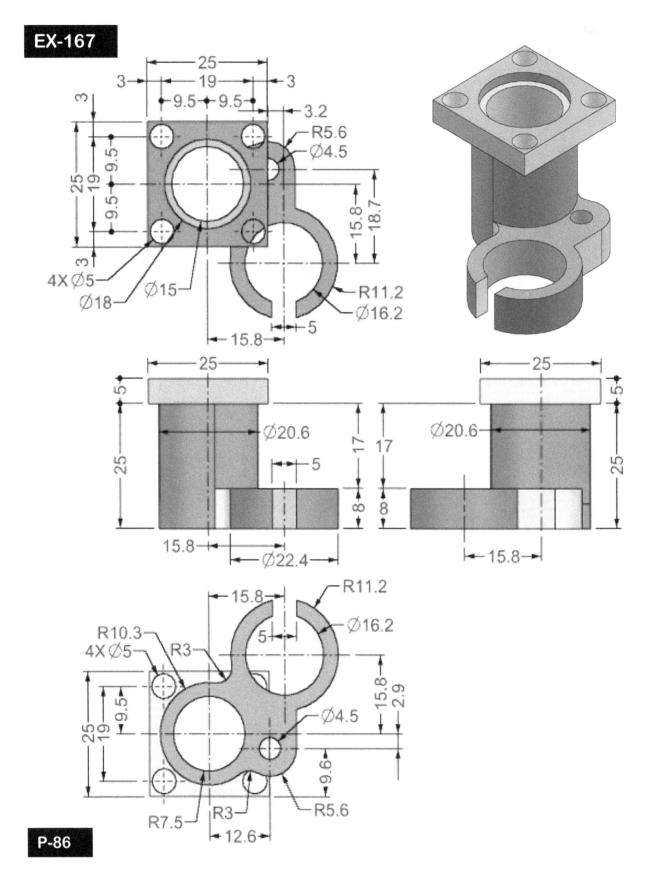

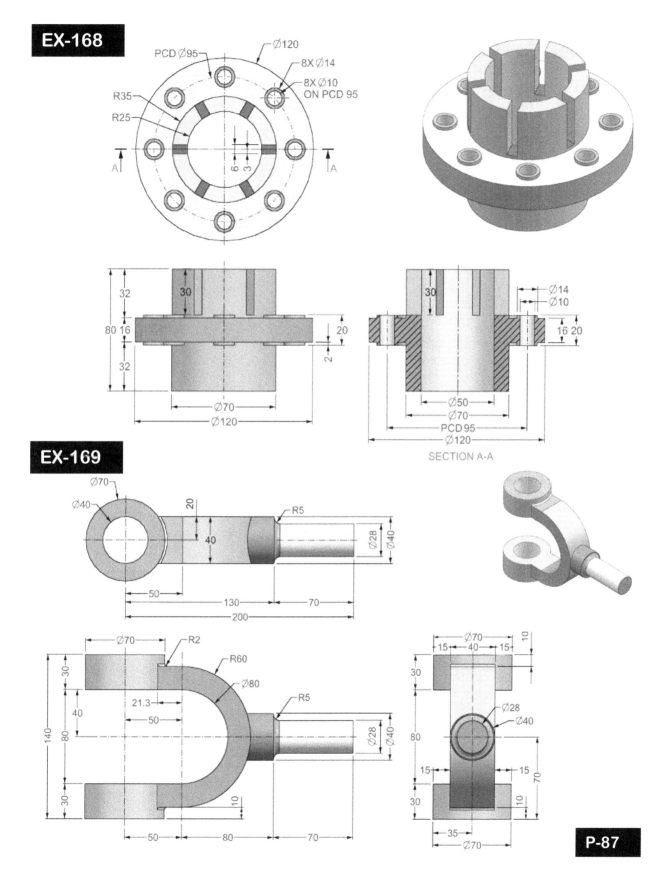

EX-168

PCD Ø95
Ø120
8X Ø14
8X Ø10
ON PCD 95
R35
R25
6
3

32
30
80 16
20
32
2

Ø70
Ø120

30
Ø14
Ø10
16 20

Ø50
Ø70
PCD 95
Ø120

SECTION A-A

EX-169

Ø70
Ø40
20
40
R5
Ø28
Ø40

50
130
70
200

Ø70
R2
R60
Ø80
R5
30
40
21.3
50
140
80
Ø28
Ø40
30
10

50
80
70

Ø70
15
40
15
10
30
30
Ø28
Ø40
80
15
15
70
30
10
35
Ø70

P-87

4X R2
3
2X Ø3
2.75 — 4.75 — Ø15 — 4.75 — 2.75
30
1
1
1
4
6

R7.5
R6.5
R2
13
8.5
R2
8.5
8.5
15
30

1
1
7.5
16
4
1
8.5
6

44 — 184 — 44
22
4X Ø23.2
92
R60
138.6
30
30
30
30
20
30
30
248
168
138.6
124
40
40
40
80
228
272

44
20 40
44
40
264
272
20
35
40

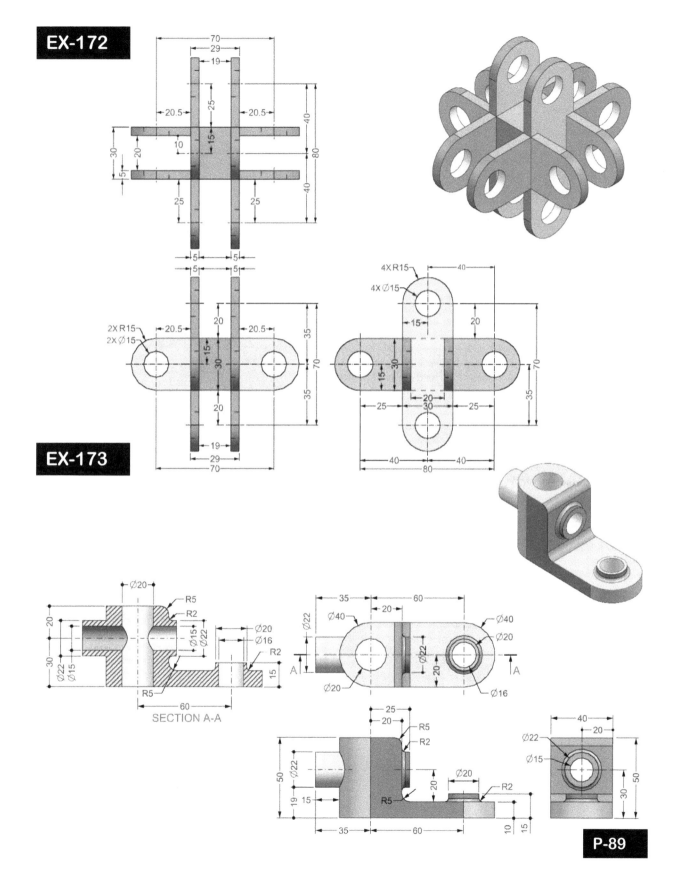

EX-172

EX-173

SECTION A-A

P-89

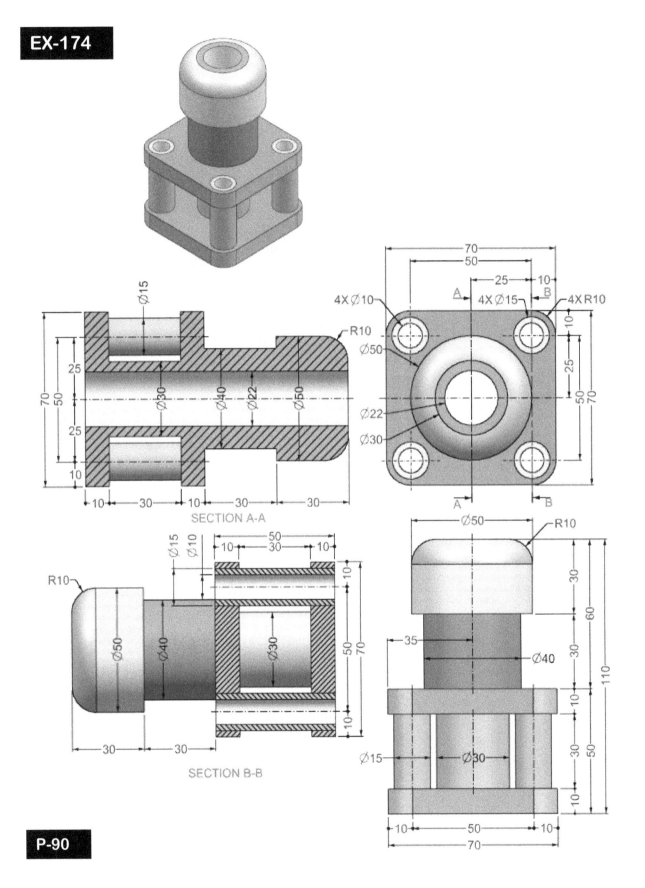

SECTION A-A

SECTION B-B

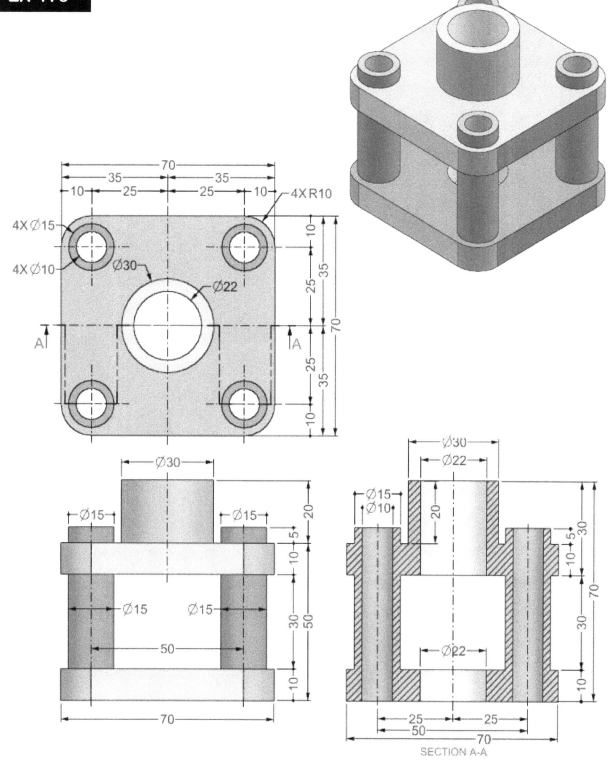

SECTION A-A

EX-176

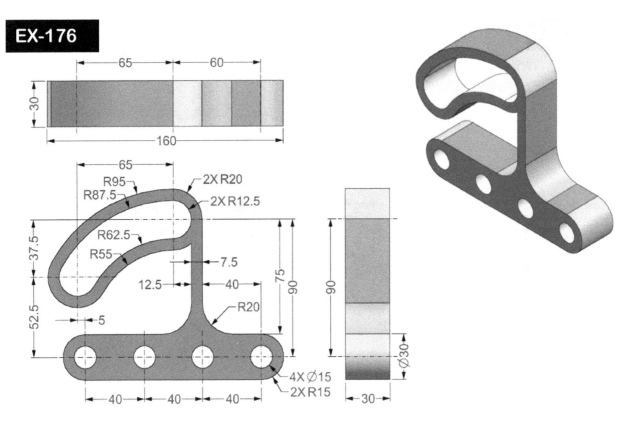

EX-177

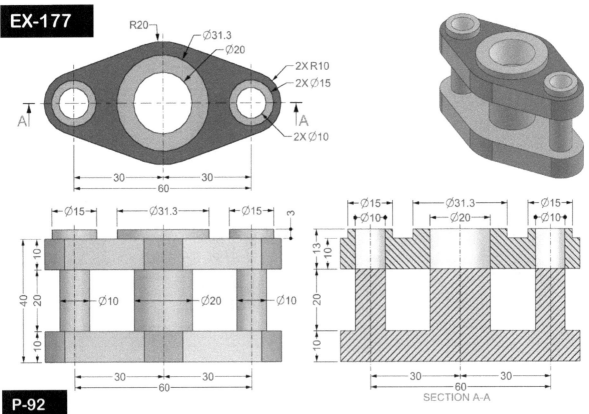

SECTION A-A

P-92

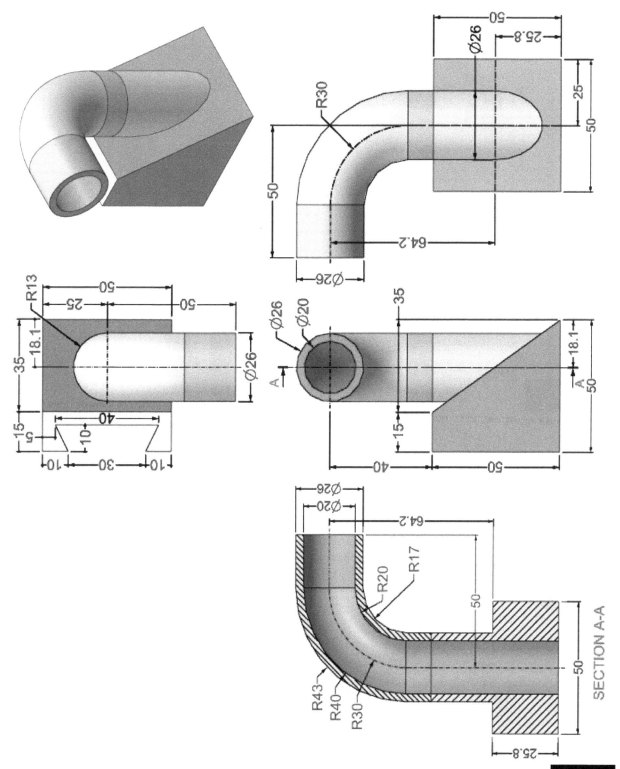

SECTION A-A

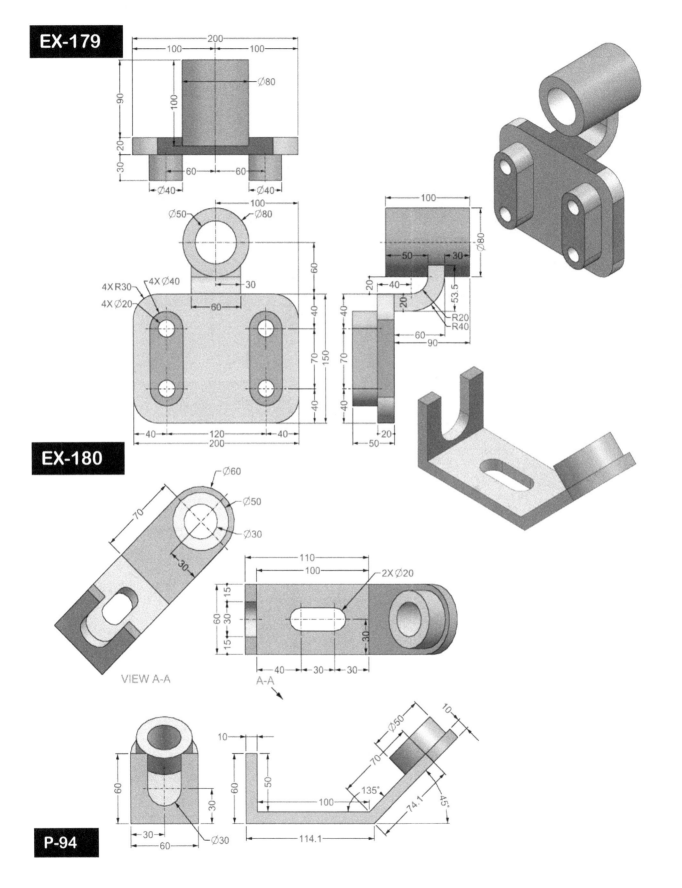

EX-179

EX-180

VIEW A-A

A-A

P-94

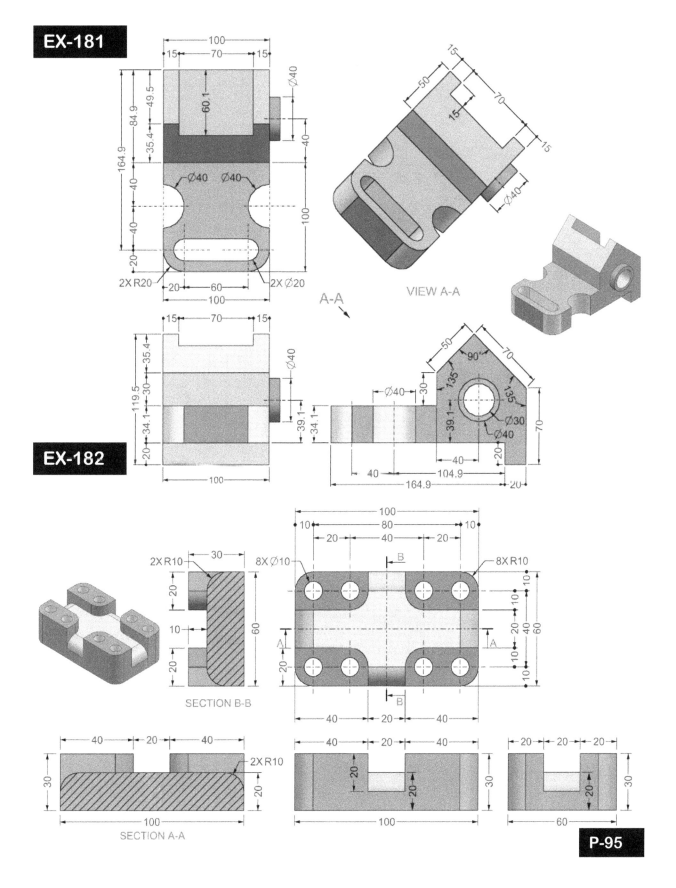

EX-181

EX-182

VIEW A-A

A-A

SECTION B-B

SECTION A-A

P-95

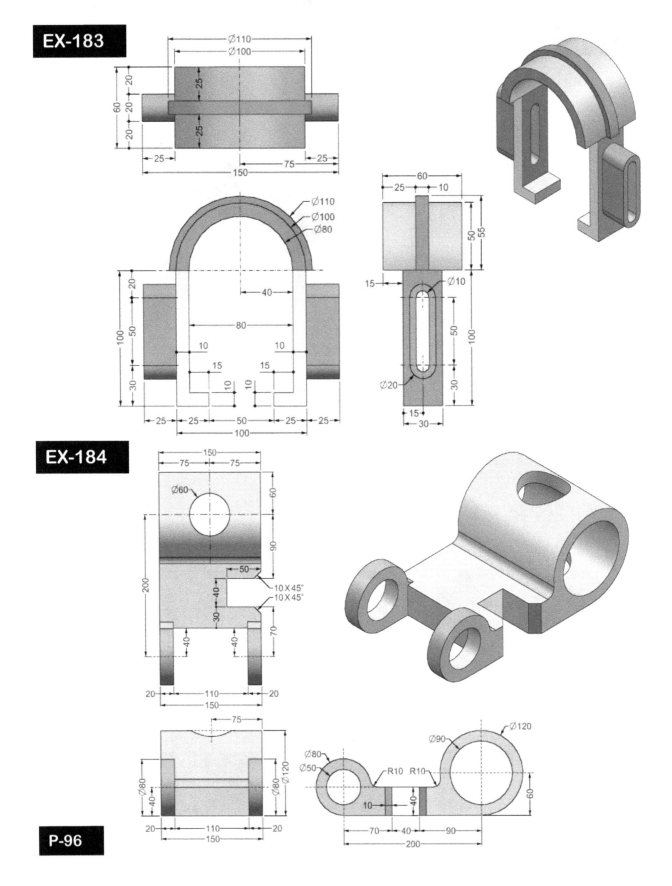

EX-183

EX-184

P-96

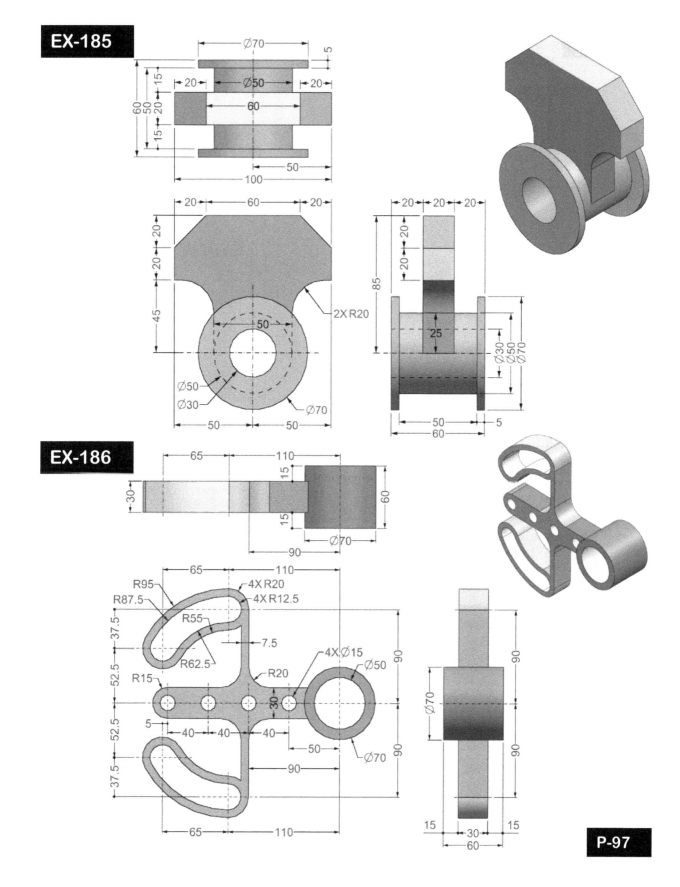

EX-185

EX-186

P-97

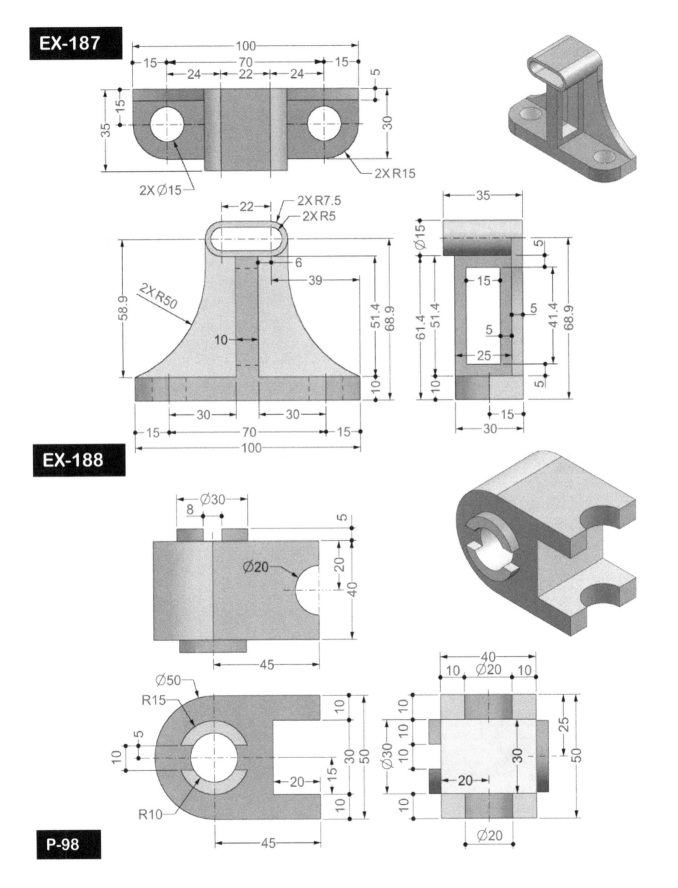

EX-187

2X∅15
2X R15
100
15 70 15
24 22 24
35
15
5
30

22 2X R7.5
2X R5
6
39
2X R50
58.9
10
51.4
68.9
10
30 30
15 70 15
100

35
∅15
5
15
5
5
25
61.4 51.4 41.4 68.9
10
5
15
30

EX-188

∅30
8
5
∅20
20
40
45

∅50
R15
5
10
R10
20
15
10
30
50
45

40
10 ∅20 10
10
10
10
10
10
∅30
20
30
25
50
∅20

P-98

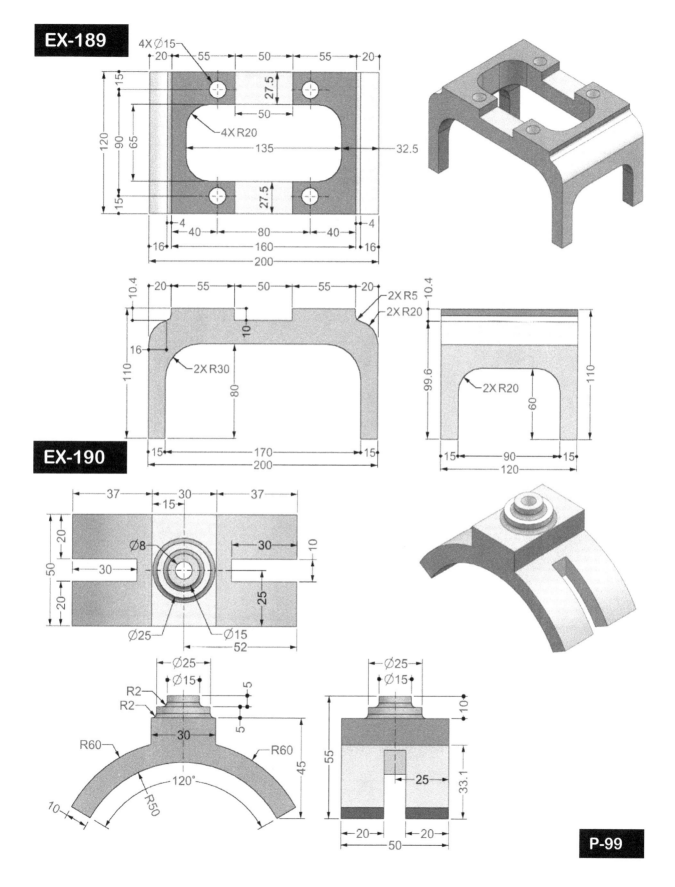

EX-189

EX-190

P-99

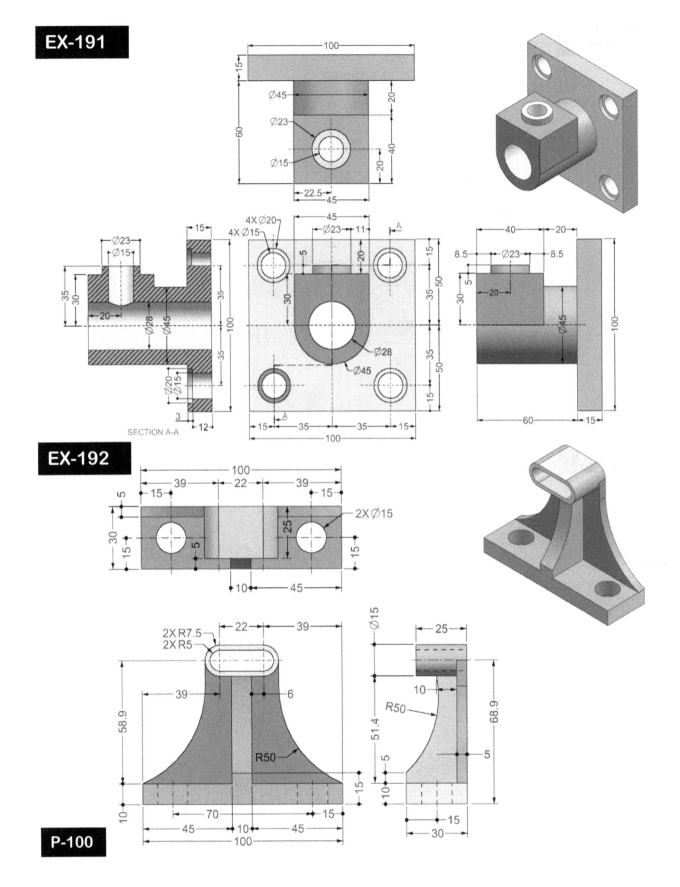

EX-191

EX-192

P-100

EX-193

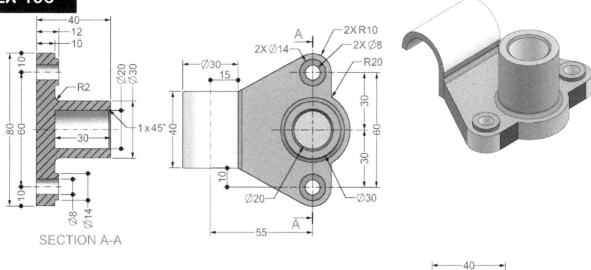

SECTION A-A

2X R10
2X Ø14
2X Ø8
R20
Ø30
15
Ø20
Ø30
40
30
60
30
10
55

Ø20
Ø30
R2
1 x 45°
40
12
10
10
80
60
30
10
Ø8
Ø14

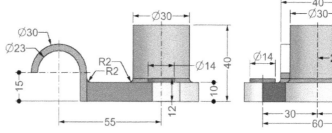

Ø30
Ø23
R2
R2
Ø30
Ø14
15
40
55
12
10

40
Ø30
20
Ø14
R3.2
40
30
30
60
10
12

EX-194

4X Ø20
150
20
110
20
55
20
40
40
15
R5
15
130
30
60
Ø120
40
30
40
70
40
35

ALL HOLES CHAMFER 2MM

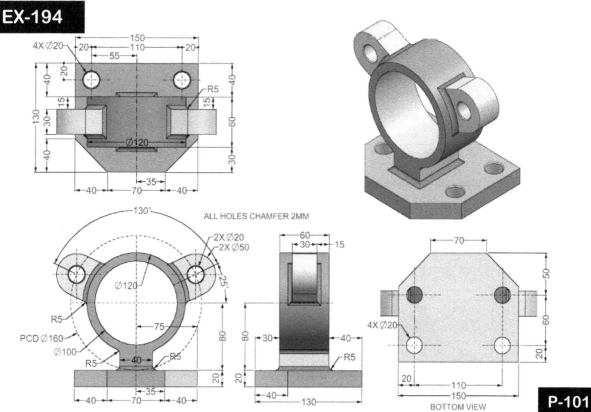

130°
2X Ø20
2X Ø50
Ø120
25°
R5
75
PCD Ø160
Ø100
80
R5
40
R5
R5
20
40
70
40
35

60
30
15
80
30
40
20
R5
20
40
130

70
50
4X Ø20
60
20
20
110
150
BOTTOM VIEW

P-101

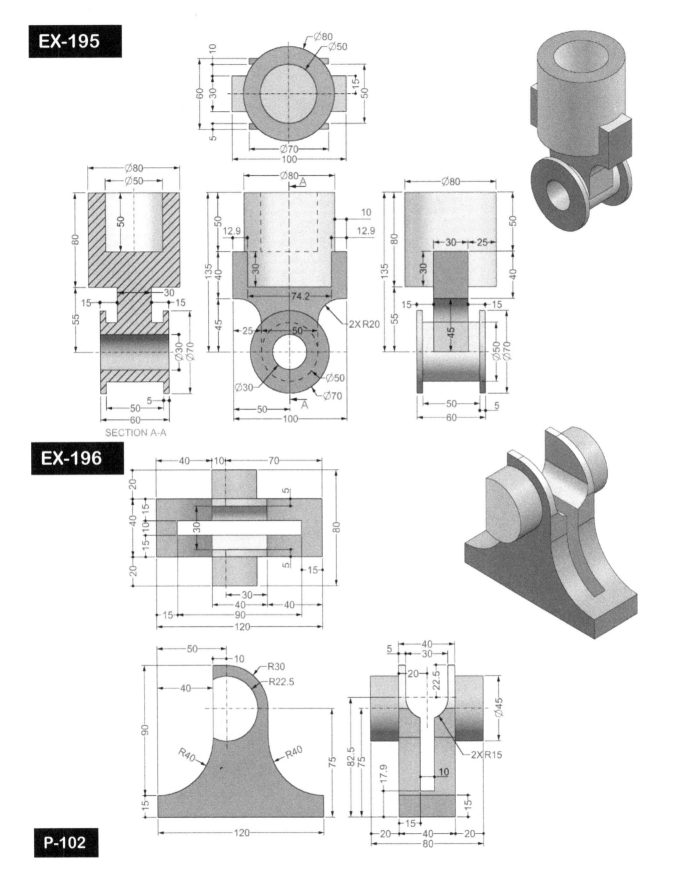

EX-195

Ø80
Ø50
10
60
30
15
50
5
Ø70
100

Ø80
Ø50
80
50
80
15
30
55
Ø30
Ø70
50
5
60
SECTION A-A

Ø80
A
50
135
40
12.9
12.9
10
30
74.2
45
25
50
2X R20
Ø30
Ø50
Ø70
50
100
A

Ø80
80
50
30
25
135
30
40
15
15
55
45
Ø50
Ø70
50
5
60

EX-196

40
10
70
20
5
40
15
10
30
80
15
5
15
30
15
20
40
40
15
90
120

50
10
R30
R22.5
40
90
R40
R40
15
120

40
5
30
20
22.5
Ø45
82.5
75
17.9
2X R15
10
15
15
20
40
20
80

P-102

EX-197

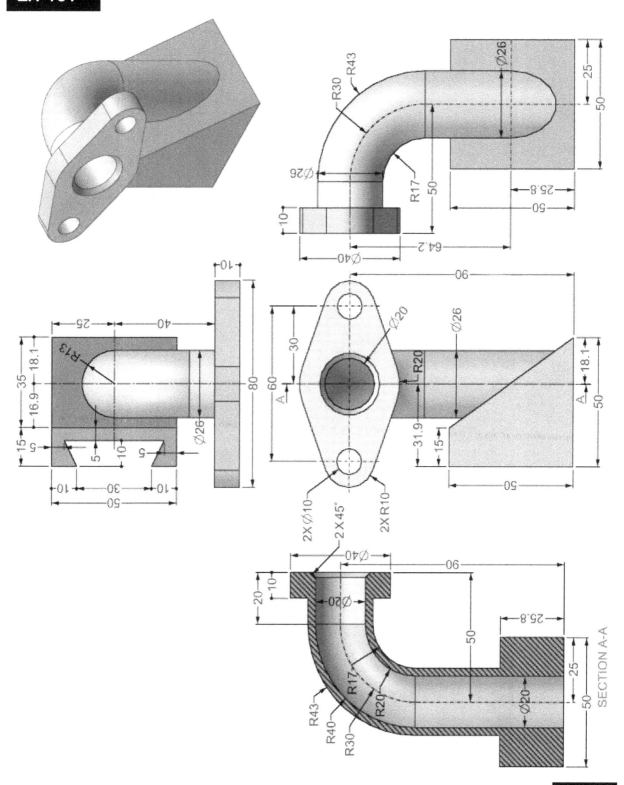

SECTION A-A

P-103

6X Ø15 THRU
ON PCD 90

Ø120
Ø50
Ø40

PCD Ø90

A

A

VIEW B-B

8X Ø10 THRU
ON PCD 54

Ø20

Ø30
Ø70

PCD Ø54

Ø120
Ø50
Ø40

15
10
Ø15
120
30

B-B

5
10
60°
60°
80
Ø20
Ø30
PCD 54
Ø10

SECTION A-A

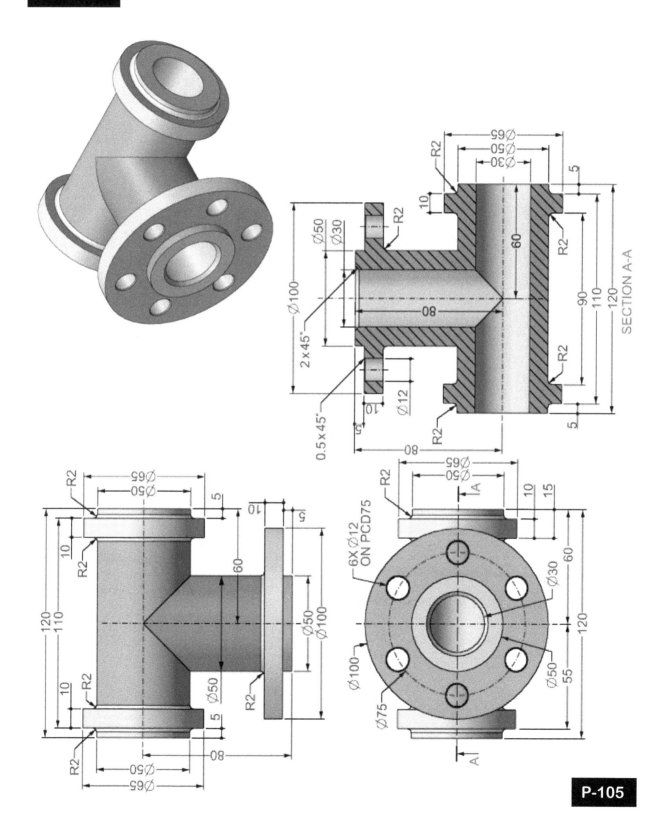

SECTION A-A

6X Ø12
ON PCD75

EX-200

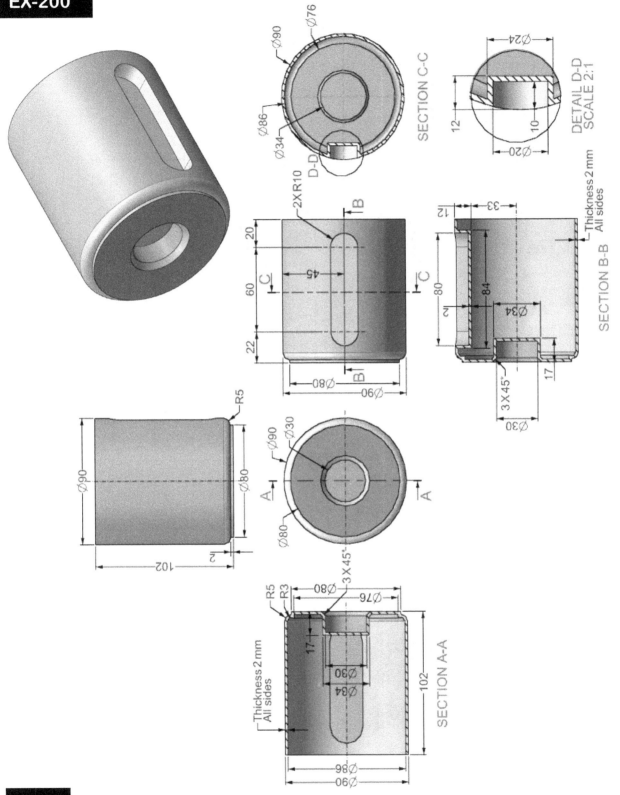

P-106

Other useful books by CADIN360

1. 150 CAD Exercises

2. AutoCAD Exercises

3. CAD Exercises

4. 50+ SolidWorks Exercises

5. SolidWorks 200 Exercises

6. Autodesk Inventor Exercises

7. Catia Exercises

8. Siemens NX Exercises

www.ingramcontent.com/pod-product-compliance
Lightning Source LLC
Chambersburg PA
CBHW080430060326
40689CB00019B/4456